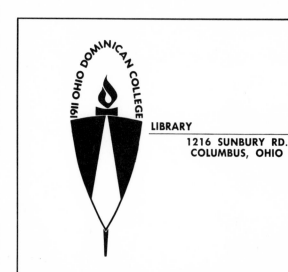

Twayne's United States Authors Series

Sylvia E. Bowman, *Editor*

INDIANA UNIVERSITY

Philip Wylie

TUSAS 285

Philip Wylie

PHILIP WYLIE

By TRUMAN FREDERICK KEEFER

TWAYNE PUBLISHERS

A DIVISION OF G. K. HALL & CO., BOSTON

Copyright © 1977 by G. K. Hall & Co.
All Rights Reserved
First Printing

Library of Congress Cataloging in Publication Data

Keefer, Truman Frederick.
  Philip Wylie.

(Twayne's United States authors series ; TUSAS 285)
  Bibliography: p. 163 - 65.
  Includes index.
  1.   Wylie, Philip, 1902 - 1971—Criticism and interpretation.
PS3545.Y46Z75   813.5'2   77-3494
ISBN 0-8057-7187-5

To Carlton Rivers, poet and scholar
and
Clarence Gohdes of Duke University

Contents

About the Author

Preface

Chronology

1. Origins   17

2. The Young Writer (1923 - 1930)   33

3. The Early 1930s (1930 - 1934)   51

4. The Magnificent *Finnley Wren*   66

5. The Late 1930s   76

6. The War Years   95

7. The Decade of Anxiety (1945 - 1955)   109

8. Years of Decline   131

9. The Last Years (1966 - 1971)   141

10. Conclusion   155

Notes and References   159

Selected Bibliography   166

Index   167

About the Author

Truman Frederick Keefer received his liberal arts education at Western Maryland College and his doctorate from Duke University, where he studied American literature. He has published *Ernest Poole* (Twayne's United States Authors Series); poetry; scholarly articles on Dickinson, Poe, Faulkner, and linguistic theory; and pieces for magazines and newspapers. Teaching at various colleges and universities since 1955, his areas of specialization include Shakespeare, creative writing, advanced composition, American Regionalism of the South and West, and the Modern British and American novel. His hobbies are color slide photography, listening to classical music, and travel at home and abroad. Dr. Keefer's current research centers on black-white relationships in contemporary life and on the psychological origins of racism.

Preface

At the age of forty, after having published nearly two score novels and novelettes, at least seventy short stories, and several dozen essays, Philip Wylie persuaded Farrar and Rinehart to issue *Generation of Vipers*. In it, he scathingly attacked his countrymen's most cherished hypocrisies and illusions about themselves; no one, not even H. L. Mencken, had ever dared to challenge with such abandon the unwritten law that certain institutions, occupations, beliefs, and personages must never be spoken of except with reverence and approval. Wylie's generalizations were so sweeping, his coverage was so complete, his language so intemperate and his contempt so infuriatingly smug that *Vipers* offended a greater number of people than any book in history.

Clergymen, educators, doctors, politicians, businessmen, and especially women of the sort he had called "Mom" counterattacked with a mindless fury and viciousness that, to the objective observer, would seem to support many of Wylie's assertions about them. But, in any case, the result of the furor was so much free publicity that Wylie at last achieved nation-wide fame—or, at least, notoriety. Even today, many books and over a quarter of a century later, he is popularly—and certainly inaccurately—known primarily for having added the term "Momism" to the language, and for just one book, which is incorrectly reputed to be dedicated exclusively to the disparagement of all women.

The time has come for a thorough examination of Wylie's works, one that will describe and evaluate his accomplishments fairly and do so without the often deliberate misrepresentations that have passed as "literary criticism." I have attempted to achieve that goal with this book, in which I combine a general, chronological account of his whole career with critical analyses of specific works. A number of Wylie's publications are given detailed treatment because, in my opinion, they are masterpieces which entitle their author to a high place among writers of this century—a view which I support with my commentaries about style, character portrayal, and dramatization of themes.

Other works were selected for discussion because they give valuable insights into the development of Wylie's skills in these areas or into the evolution of the central themes of his works. Because I have found that certain traumatic experiences in Wylie's personal life and his fascination with the discoveries of modern science, especially in biology and psychology, were key factors in those processes, I have given particular attention to their influence. Unfortunately, because of limitations on the length of the present volume, I have not been able to examine such aspects of Wylie's writing as style or biographical echoes as fully as I might, and I have also had to focus almost exclusively upon the major works.

The conclusions which I have drawn about Wylie's literary career are based on the evidence uncovered in a long and systematic examination of a substantial portion of his published work. When the project was begun in 1966, the plan was to read everything which Wylie had written in order to trace the evolution of his ideas and the development of his powers of expression and—incidentally—to determine whether he had ever produced anything as noteworthy as *Vipers*. The long lists of books and the number of pieces listed in the standard indexes were somewhat intimidating, yet the task, though large, appeared to have discernible limits. But, in fact, the majority of his publications, being in "popular" magazines, had never been catalogued, and these included a large number of novels. Thus the "working bibliography," compiled from the files of Wylie's literary agent and the records of the magazines still in existence, as well as surveys of back issues of defunct periodicals, was twice as long as expected. In some cases, it was impossible or impractical to obtain copies of certain materials; not even the Library of Congress, for example, has complete files of every pulp magazine ever issued. Nevertheless, this survey of the Wylie canon can be described as reasonably thorough.

The other major source of information for this book was Philip Wylie himself. During a five-year period, he patiently answered countless questions about his life and works—often in letters that ran to twenty pages of single-spaced typing and twice in tape recorded interviews that ran on for two or three days and nights at a time. The biographical data, background information on specific books, and especially his views about the creative process were of inestimable value and could not have been derived from any other source. In all of his communications, he made a genuine effort not to influence the researcher in his favor. In fact, he often declared that only a full disclosure of all the facts, one that included his worst mistakes and flaws, could make any significant contribution to the pursuit of truth, and he carried out that belief with his characteristic thoroughness. I was left with the ineradicable conviction that here was an honest man—and that it was his dedication to truth (along with his fundamental generosity) which had led him to sacrifice many precious hours that he needed to spend on his own work.

Certain other people also deserve mention for their help in the preparation of this book. Mrs. Frederica Wylie, Max Wylie, and Karen Wylie Pryor made important comments on my manuscript. Dorothy Olding, the literary agent, provided lists of everything sold through the Harold Ober agency and estimates of the total sales of all of the books. Carol Leroy Peck bravely transcribed tape recordings and my handwritten manuscripts. Greatest is my debt of gratitude to Harold Nadel, my colleague and friend, who single-handedly cut my thousand page manuscript into a publishable whole.

Truman Frederick Keefer

Franklin, Ohio, 1976

Chronology

1902   Philip Gordon Wylie born May 12 in North Beverly, Mass.

1907   Family moved to Cleveland. Mother died in childbirth.

1909   Moved to Delaware, Ohio.

1912   Burst appendix in March nearly killed young Wylie.

1914   Moved to Montclair, New Jersey, in May.

1920   Exploration in Canadian wilderness.

1922   Suspended from Princeton in March, 1922, because of low grades.

1922-
1923   Readmitted to Princeton. Courses in physics, geology, evolution stimulated interest in science. "Personality conflict" with literature professor ended college career.

1923   Took position with Bernays and Thorson, public relations firm, in July.

1924   Established own successful advertising agency with help of John G. Hamilton. Scandal created by bastardy charge made by Henrietta Hammond in October. In December, joined the staff assembled by Harold Ross to found the *New Yorker*.

1927   Wrote verse and pulp magazine stories. *Titan* (renamed *Gladiator*) accepted by Knopf. Met Sally Ondeck, Powers model and divorcée, and visited France with her.

1928   *Heavy Laden*. First "fables" published in *Vanity Fair*. Married Sally, April 17. Six-month honeymoon in France.

1929   *Babes and Sucklings*.

1930   *Gladiator*. *Blondy's Boy Friend* by "Leatrice Homesley." Met Edwin Balmer; began lengthy collaboration; became regular contributor to *Redbook*. First sales in November to the "slick" magazines, *Saturday Evening Post* and *Collier's*.

1931   *The Murderer Invisible*. *Footprint of Cinderella*. *Five Fatal Words* with Balmer. First Hollywood stint as scenario writer with Paramount.

1932   Karen, only child, born May 14. *When Worlds Collide* (with Balmer), magazine publication in September. *The Savage Gentleman*. End of sexual union with Sally.

1933   Visited nuclear physics laboratories at California Institute of Technology.

1934   *After Worlds Collide* (with Balmer). *Finnley Wren. Golden Hoard* (with Balmer). First publication in the exclusive *Cosmopolitan* in September.

1935   *The Smiling Corpse,* written with Bernard Bergman.

1936   *As They Reveled. The Shield of Silence* (with Balmer). *Too Much of Everything. Second Honeymoon* (in *Redbook*). Trip with brother, Edmund, to Russia in June. Edmund killed in Warsaw, June 27. Philip paralyzed for a month from cholera. Began visits to analyst, Archibald Strong, to find cure for depression and alcoholism.

1937   *Smoke Across the Moon* and *Home from the Hills* in *Redbook*. Divorced from Sally. Met Frederica Ballard.

1938   Marriage to "Ricky" Ballard on April 7. *An April Afternoon. Profile of a Prodigal* in *Redbook*.

1939   "Widow Voyage," first Crunch and Des story, in *Saturday Evening Post* on June 10.

1940   Chairman of Dade County chapter of Committee to Defend America. Worked in Stop Hitler campaign. *The Army Way* with William Muir. *The Big Ones Get Away*—fishing stories. *No Scandal!* in *Redbook*.

1941   *Salt Water Daffy* (stories). Service in Office of Facts and Figures, December, 1941, until May, 1942.

1942   *The Other Horseman.*

1943   *Generation of Vipers. Corpses at Indian Stones.*

1944   *Fish and Tin Fish* (stories). *Night Unto Night.* In February began column, "Off My Chest."

1947   *An Essay on Morals.*

1948   *Crunch and Des.* Became a director of the Lerner Laboratories in Bimini, a biological research center.

1949   *Opus 21.* Helped persuade Senator Brien McMahon to urge Harry Truman to build H-bomb.

1950   Advisor to Gordon Dean, Chairman of Atomic Energy Commission.

1951   *The Disappearance. Three to Be Read.*

1953   *Denizens of the Deep* (essays).

1954   *Tomorrow! The Best of Crunch and Des.*

1956   Trip around world, January 31 to end of April. *Treasure Cruise* (stories). *The Answer.*

1957   *The Innocent Ambassadors.* Start of long period of nonproductivity and of use of amphetamines to lift depressed moods.

1963   *Triumph.* Became affiliated with Doubleday. Barely escaped death from fire in home in Rushford, New York.

1964   Sold Florida home to meet debts.

1965   *They Both Were Naked.*

1968   *The Magic Animal.*

1969   *The Spy Who Spoke Porpoise.*

1970   Heart attack in October. Bed rest for six months.

1971   *The Sons and Daughters of Mom. Los Angeles: A. D. 2017,* television play and novel. Died in Miami, October 25, of heart failure.

1972   *The End of the Dream* published posthumously.

CHAPTER 1

Origins

THE literary works of Philip Wylie, like those of any
reputable author, can be understood and appreciated even if
the reader knows nothing about the artist's life. Nevertheless, many
of the facts about his family background, upbringing, and personal
experiences help to explain the particular nature of his talent, the
origin and development of his esthetic, moral, and philosophical
views, and even the factors that produced the inner-directed,
iconoclastic, highly individual personality which makes itself felt so
unmistakably in his writings. In such background material, we may
also find the real-life sources of the events and characters in some of
Wylie's works of fiction, and from them we can determine readily
the degree to which the writer was a transmuter of reality rather
than a recorder of it. What follows, then, is a survey of the formative years of Philip Wylie.

I *Family Background*

Our subject's ancestors, the Edwards and the Wylie families,
came to New England from Scotland, near Aberdeen, in the
seventeenth and early eighteenth century, respectively. The
members of both lines were marked by energy, intellectual power,
determination, and, apparently, absolute certainty about the val-
idity of their own religious and philosophical views. It is not surprising to find that Wylie's mother was a collateral descendant of
the Puritan genius, Jonathan Edwards (Wylie's tenth great-
grandfather), and a relative of the Henry Ward Beecher family, or
that present-day Wylies claim Aaron Burr as a distant, if misguided,
relative in their paternal lineage. These archetypal early Americans,
after crossing an ocean to find freedom for the practice of their
religion, moved westward on the continent in search of more
materialistic goals; and, by the late nineteenth century, they were

geographically and culturally a part of the Great Midwest. Edna Edwards, the writer's mother, was born in 1876 in Sibley, Iowa; his father, Edmund Melville Wylie, born in 1875 in Coulterville, Illinois, grew up in Minnesota and North Dakota. Their son, Philip, would, therefore, like many writers of his generation, be a product of and a rebel against the last great Puritan Establishment in America.

The grandparents on both sides strongly affected Wylie by genetic inheritance and example. Ira C. Edwards was a successful insurance salesman, an enthusiastic sportsman and fisherman, and the author of the lyrics of many published popular songs. From him, Wylie believed, he inherited his own business ability, his fascination with nature, and his verbal facility—and, possibly, a very un-Puritan delight in the visible world and its sensual pleasures. Grandmother Edwards was, reportedly, a kind and unusually permissive woman who was certainly not a believer in discipline for children. David and Elizabeth (Morrison) Wylie, by contrast, are more familiar types. He was a serious-minded farmer, a general store manager, and the part-owner of some flour and grist mills. His wife was a harsh, cheerless, intolerant, and fanatical Covenanter, whose dedication to her views was surpassed only by her determination to impose them on others. Between 1907 and 1911, she and Mrs. Edwards took turns caring for the three Wylie children after their mother's death. Her efforts at correcting their behavior were unnecessarily strict and, worse, totally undermined by Grandmother Edwards' laxness. Undoubtedly, the start of Philip's lifelong hatred of domineering women and of evangelical Christianity can be attributed to her actions, which made his childhood miserable.

Wylie's mother was the source of his greatest talents and the molder of his fundamental view of life. He inherited her intelligence (she had attended Hamline College in Minnesota and met her future husband there) and her facility in verbal expression. She had, for example, the ability to compose effortlessly in rhyme, and she also published a number of popular sentimental novels, including *The Blue Valley Feud* and, in 1905, *The Ward of the Sewing Circle*.[1] Had she lived a normal life span, she might also have passed on to him her cheerful optimism. A warm and affectionate woman like her own mother, she did give him a happy and secure early childhood. But when she died suddenly while giving birth to her fourth child, Philip was only five and a half years old, a very impressionable age. Consequently, he carried emotional scars for the rest of his life: an abiding sense of irreparable loss; a nagging awareness of his own vulnerability in an insecure world; perhaps, too, a smoldering rage against the pain and meaninglessness of the suffering inflicted on him.

Unlike Philip's siblings, Max and Verona, he was old enough to remember his mother clearly, and, with the stubbornness of a child, he refused to forget her. When his father married Wilmina Kiskaddon four years later, he regarded the act as a betrayal of Edna's memory and never accepted his stepmother as a substitute for his real mother. As a result, he condemned himself to a lonely, motherless childhood and, as an adult, to a hopeless search for a woman who would give him the kind of love which had been missing earlier. Furthermore, by the time he became an adult, his increasingly idealized picture of Edna had become the standard by which he judged all women and, inevitably, the cause of great disappointment. It is no surprise that the kind of female he hated most was "Mom," the antithesis of the maternal ideal, or that Ricky Ballard, the woman with whom he finally found a measure of happiness, resembled Edna Wylie in personality, appearance, and the sound of her voice.[2]

Wylie's emotional attachment to Edna's memory had other effects on him as an adult. It caused him to be overly protective to women and to avoid "taking advantage" of them, especially sexually; he was proud that he had never "deflowered" a virgin. Unfortunately, his attitude often encouraged women to exploit him and, in consequence, produced the bitterness found in books like *Vipers*. His reverence for his mother also helps to explain his advocacy of equal rights for women, including the freedom to have pre-marital and extra-marital affairs—a position that would have shocked his Victorian parent.[3] Probably the most important consequence of his esteem for Edna was that he genuinely liked women and, unlike most men, tried to understand them and their behavior patterns. The knowledge that he gained explains why the female characters in his best fiction are incomparably convincing.

Wylie's complex relationship with his father, distorted by misunderstanding and hatred, affected his life, attitudes, and literary career even more than did his love for his mother—and did so in ways that were very unpleasant for everyone. The son's earliest memories of his father set the pattern:[4] circumcised without an anesthetic at eighteen months, he blamed the pain and fear on his parent, who had held down the struggling, terrified child. When Philip was perhaps six, the Reverend Wylie tried to teach him to swim by throwing him into Lake Erie; Philip nearly drowned. He also seems, with the obscure reasoning of a child, to have blamed his father for the death of Edna in 1907; and, when the grief-stricken widower immersed himself in his work, he unsuspectingly deepened the gulf between himself and his equally unhappy youngster, who more than ever needed the comfort of a loving parent. Four years later, when the attractive, talented, twenty-two-year-old Wilmina Kiskaddon became his stepmother, the child was further embittered because he resented a happiness in which he had no part, for, even at that early age, he was aware that the couple were "tremendously physically in love." The alienation worsened when he reached puberty; by that time, Wilmina had become the constant object of his sexual fantasies, and his father was now, to him, a hated, successful sexual rival.

But the main and constant cause of the son's animosity was Reverend Wylie's profession. Like most ministers' sons, Philip was personally aware that his father did not live up to the Christian ideals which he advocated in his pulpit. With the unforgiving harshness of the young, Philip condemned, as conscious hypocrisy, acts which really showed only forgiveable human weakness. Still, life with Edmund Wylie was not easy. He lavished his time on the needs of his congregation, rather than his family. The moral lapses of the children were duly reported by the father on Sunday as they sat, a captive audience, in his church. Punishment was occasionally more direct: Philip never forgot that his father once beat him to un-consciousness for repeating a vulgar jingle heard at school. The significance of the event was not lost on the boy: the spiritual leader of a religion that proclaimed the compassion and forgiveness of Christ, but battered his own son in uncontrollable fury over a harmless indiscretion, was despicable—and so was his religion. Philip swore then that his father and his religion would receive their proper reward, and in time they did, in slashing portraits of the man and the faith in book after book, from *Heavy Laden* and *Finnley Wren* to *Vipers* itself. Thus, out of a sordid quarrel tinged with Oedipal conflict was born the violent anticlericism which was to become his trademark.

The irony in this situation was that the Reverend Wylie's liberal views and example as a seeker after truth would probably have propelled his son into militant atheism even if they had been friends. Edmund Wylie did not accept the Bible as the literal Word of God, was opposed to all doctrines which led to intolerance of the beliefs of others, and believed in the right of the individual to reject those parts of official doctrine about which he had genuine doubts. He himself had left the Congregational Church of his parents and became a Presbyterian despite the opposition of his mother, with whom he waged continual verbal battles. He voiced his views from his pulpit and challenged his listeners to examine their own beliefs. On one occasion he reproved young Philip for accepting, without questioning, the ideas presented in a Sunday School lesson.

Of course, the minister was certain that freedom of inquiry would lead to a truer understanding of Christ's message and a strengthening of Christianity. He could not foresee that, in the age of modern science, the first victim of that inquiry would be revealed religion itself. Nor could he have guessed that Philip, infused since infancy with his father's missionary zeal, would promote with equal energy the truth which *he* had found. Nevertheless, the Reverend Wylie had given to his son his own dedication to the search for the meaning and purpose of life and for an ethical system based on that fundamental reality. As a result, Wylie was never to be contented with the idea that the universe is a meaningless collection of phenomena. At first, he hoped to find a new religion in the discoveries of the physical sciences; by the 1930s he had turned instead to those of psychology, to Freud and then to Jung. The search resulted in the writing of *Vipers* and *An Essay on Morals* and, near the end of his career, *The Magic Animal*, where he expressed his final position. In all, his life and his serious writings were a search for a religion, a fact which, ironically, the elder Wylie recognized before his son did. As he said to Philip after *Vipers* appeared, "You're a hell of a lot better preacher than I ever was." And he was not referring merely to the techniques of the sermon which the book employed or to its expression of outrage at moral deficiencies.

Many years passed before Wylie was able to gain any perspective on his relationship with his father. When he did, he realized that he had inherited or otherwise acquired many of his parent's qualities: intelligence, a love of learning, a gift for verbal expression, physical vitality and seemingly endless energy, self-reliance and determination verging on stubbornness. These were all qualities that made possible his later spectacular literary career, but they also had made conflict inevitable between father and son. The latter, after years spent in psychoanalysis, finally saw that he had genuinely admired and respected his father and his accomplishments but that his own ego had demanded that he compete successfully with him and win his approval. When he could not do either, the only recourse was rebellion and willful misbehavior. Although he had told himself that he was an idealist in honest revolt against the prudery and secret viciousness of the Victorians (which, in part, he was), he had not understood that some of his "hell-raising" was motivated by little more than a child's need to get his parent's attention.

Wylie, however, had never doubted the importance to him of his father's unconventional attempts to educate him. For instance, he taught him to read when he was five—primarily to give the lonely child something to distract his mind—and had thus established a life-long insatiable desire for the printed word that educated him far better than his formal education ever did. Philip was allowed to read anything he could understand, even novels, because his father believed in "the freedom to know," which, as his son would argue in the 1950s, is the one freedom on which all others are based. Another of his father's projects was vocabulary-building: for years he required his sons to learn a new word each day. The direct result was that Philip's limitless supply of words and his fondness for unusual ones became an extraordinary aspect of his style as a writer. E. M. Wylie put into operation some other radical ideas about education. When the boy was nine, he gave him a detailed, complete, and accurate explanation of how human beings reproduced themselves; the information not only spared young Wylie the feelings of guilt which are spawned by ignorance but also enabled him to see later on, and to expose in *Vipers,* just how foolish his fellow Americans were in their attempts to keep sex a secret that could not be discussed in public and helped him to understand how the secrecy had created a society that was close to a mental breakdown.

Of Reverend Wylie's good qualities, the most impressive was his physical and moral courage. In 1913, when he led a campaign to close the saloons in Delaware, Ohio, he did not seem disturbed by threats of death or by a real bullet fired at him in the dark. In the same year, he saved nineteen trapped people during a flood by swimming with a rope through currents that had drowned earlier rescuers. In 1917, he went to France with the Young Men's Christian Association, served in the front lines as a chaplain, and once narrowly escaped death. The elder Wylie's example of courage explains in part Philip's predilection for never avoiding fights against superior forces—and also his capacity to survive the unending losses, defeats, and disappointments of his life. This gift was, certainly, his father's most valuable legacy.

II *Childhood*

Those who remember Philip Wylie in his earlier years recall that he was different from his peers. Perhaps because of his grief after his mother's death, he became increasingly introspective; reading a great deal also encouraged his tendency to live within himself; and so, even as a boy he came to prefer being alone so that he could think without interruption.[5] In this sense, his childhood was a good preparation for his career as a writer, a life which would consist mostly of long periods of creativity in solitary rooms.

His reading included the major boys' books of the time. His favorites were Jonathan Swift's *Gulliver's Travels*, Daniel Defoe's *Robinson Crusoe*, Lew Wallace's *Ben Hur*, Jules Verne's *Twenty Thousand Leagues Under the Sea*, and Johann Wyss' *Swiss Family Robinson*. By 1912 he had explored the works of H. G. Wells, Edgar A. Poe, and Edgar Rice Burroughs, the "Oz" books of Frank Baum, and the Tom Swift tales of Edward Stratemeyer. Philip quite early displayed his creative talent as a story-teller by enthralling his brother with his own versions of famous stories, and, in his later years, he reflected the influence of writers like Wells and Verne in his own works of fantasy and science fiction.

As Wylie grew older, the books he read encouraged his natural tendency to be self-reliant intellectually. He learned to think, to pursue lines of research to satisfy his endless curiosity, to accept nothing on faith. Consequently, he could not conceal a certain arrogance. Adults, particularly, could not bear his "know-it-all" attitude, especially when it was based on documentation, sound logic, and common sense. They were only the first of literally millions who would experience that feeling.

As a child, Wylie was small for his age and somewhat lacking in athletic ability—facts that had important consequences. One was that he seldom took part in such sports as football or baseball, and, instead of growing out of his solitary ways, became even more inclined to spend his time reading and daydreaming his way through stories of his own invention—becoming, in other words, proficient in the same creative process that he would use when he became a writer. Another effect was that he, like many unathletic children, grew up filled with envy of athletes and with an obsessive need to emulate their feats. Part of that need was satisfied in childhood by daydreams in which he pictured himself performing heroic deeds of physical prowess. It found a similar outlet in adulthood in some of the stories he wrote, tales in which characters like the man of super-strength, Hugo Danner (in *Gladiator*) or those immortal pugilists, Crunch and Des, acted out his private fantasies and brought their creator an immense popular following among readers who shared his need for vicarious achievements.

Young Wylie was not, however, satisfied with imagined victories; he also desired to prove himself in the real world. He made it a rule never to back away from a fight, particularly when the opponent was much larger than he; and, when he battled, he did so with complete disregard for his own well-being and with the pugnacity he would show later in life when he would challenge such "sacred cows" as Christianity, the ethics of business, and the American Mom. Mostly, however, he competed against himself. For example, he taught himself to swim and dive by practicing alone in a dangerous flooded quarry; he learned there the patience and self-discipline that would enable him to develop his literary talent and to overcome the frustrations that he would encounter as a free-lance writer.

During these early years, Philip was constantly in touch with nature in a way that few young Americans today can possibly be. In later years, he advised parents to make any sacrifices necessary to give their offspring a childhood away from the cities. He would assert that much of the anxiety and violence of modern man is caused by his being raised in hostile, unhealthy, restrictive, unnatural urban environments; and he believed that the American adults' fascination with games, sports, and the whole cult of youthfulness was an indication of their unfulfilled need for a real childhood that had been denied them.[6] As might be expected, Wylie became one of the first to attack the destruction of the environment by technological "advances"—in part because he knew from his study of biology that man was on the way to destroying the biosphere itself, but initially because he could recall clearly the happiest days of his life, when there were clear streams and skies, when automobiles were few, and when the population was not taking over the living space that other life forms were entitled to.

For Wylie, childhood came to an end—in a psychological sense—in the spring of 1912, when he nearly died from a burst appendix and peritonitis. When the boy had first complained of stomach pains, his stepmother had called in a chiropractor, who, for four days, methodically kneaded the stomach and, of course, burst the infected organ. At last Philip was taken to a hospital, but the infection was so widespread that the doctors—as would happen on other occasions in Wylie's life—announced his imminent death. Only at the insistence of Reverend Wylie did they continue the operation. The father stayed with his son, watching their desperate efforts, and perhaps, by his presence, gave the boy the will to live. After four more operations and a year of convalescence, he was recovered in body, a miracle of human vitality.[7] But he had known physical pain of such intensity and duration that his entire outlook on life was changed. Gone was his innocence of suffering; in its place was a certainty that life had more of the same waiting for him (as, indeed, it did) and that it would be no easier to bear the next time. He had experienced the mindless terror of facing his own death, and that, too, was unforgettable.

Understandably, many of Wylie's books show the direct influence of his terrible exposure to death and physical pain at an impressionable age. He actually used the abdominal operation only once, in *Heavy Laden*, but *Opus 21* and *Night Unto Night* both center on main characters who must face horrible ends, one by cancer and the other by epileptic convulsions caused by deterioration of the nervous system. Only a writer with personal experience of this kind of situation could have given fiction such frightening authenticity. The episode when Wylie was ten also explains his belief, set forth in *Vipers* and *An Essay on Morals*, that man had invented all the lies he calls religion when he discovered that he was an animal doomed to personal extinction. Having known the full extent of the terror of death, he could readily understand why people would seize upon any illogical absurdity that would promise them escape from that fear—and why they would fight so hard to retain that belief.

It is also obvious that one of Wylie's literary trademarks—his sickening accounts of mutilation and injury—as in *Vipers*, *Finnley Wren*, and *Tomorrow!*—is not an attempt at gratuitous sensationalism but, rather, a reflection of his understandable life-long obsession with such matters. In fact, even in supposedly "non-serious" works like his Crunch and Des stories, we often find an underlying tone of seriousness, an echo of his conception of life as a sequence of events that—both literally and figuratively—rend and scar their victims. It is therefore no exaggeration to say that, at the age of ten, Wylie had already found his most compelling theme.

Psychologists have observed that survivors of nearly fatal accidents look for—and find—an explanation of why they escaped. Apparently the mind cannot cope with the idea that chance had anything to do with one's escape, and therefore these people insist that either supernatural intervention (God, fate, luck) or some personal quality preserved them. Young Wylie unquestioningly accepted the view of the doctors that his will to live, his determination to fight on when hope was gone, had saved his life. As an adult, he never relinquished that belief, and, in fact, it became the basis of his philosophy of life—that one must always find the courage to bear what must be borne. The alternative is certain defeat in cases where victory might be salvaged through endurance to the end, and loss of self-respect when that only can be preserved in the general ruin.

Wylie lived during his next sixty years through many terrifying and pain-filled experiences, usually with a bravery that amazed others and especially himself, because he knew that each new display of coolness and endurance had come only after a long struggle with his fears. This hard-earned knowledge is reflected in the exploits of a number of his fictional characters. Men like Crunch Adams (especially when he reaches middle age), Finnley Wren, "Phil Wylie" in Opus 21, and Ring Grove of The Spy Who Spoke Porpoise are not brave by reflex or nature: each has lonely hours when he is very much afraid. But ultimately each steels himself with the conviction that he has no choice except to be steadfast. The fact that these heroes are possessed of weaknesses makes them believable—and so intensely human that their portraits are among the best Wylie ever drew.

The five crucial years in the childhood of Wylie, those spent in Delaware, Ohio, suddenly ended in 1914, when Reverend Wylie accepted an offer to become the pastor of the new Central Presbyterian Church in Montclair, New Jersey. In May, the family departed on their five-day journey in a new Overland touring car, and Philip did not return for more than thirty years. Wylie himself later regarded the move to Montclair and the nearby New York City as an escape from the provincialism and hypocrisy of Middle America and Main Street, and he for years echoed this theme in his fiction.

But, in fact, like most products of the Midwest, he carried with him a complete set of "old-fashioned" values—his belief in individualism, in self-reliance, and in hard work as a prerequisite for success, in a free but responsible system of private enterprise, and in the pursuit of happiness in a free society. These ideals made him the satirist and social critic of *Vipers*, who attacked Communism, Socialism, and Fascism, big government, irresponsible labor unionism, all manner of educational, economic, and social panaceas that restricted freedom, and every evil which tried to undermine his dream of an ideal America. All of his years in the East never altered his fundamental Midwestern ideals, and it is therefore completely ironical that the most vitriolic response to *Vipers* would come from the area which had produced him, where many wondered aloud what kind of "foreign agitator" he was and why he didn't "go back where he came from."

III *Adolescence*

Montclair, New Jersey, gave Wylie educational opportunities he might never have had in Delaware, Ohio. When he entered the local public school system, he was placed in a new experimental class, composed entirely of students of high intelligence, and kept there until his graduation five years later. The mental stimulation given by his gifted classmates was an important element in his development even though he continued to be a loner. Since the curriculum was flexible and innovative rather than dedicated to rote learning in traditional subjects, it was ideally suited to Wylie's temperament, although he in fact applied himself only in subjects that interested him, spent a great deal of time in extracurricular activities such as magic shows, and thus received only average grades. He always insisted that his private research into the making of fireworks, rockets, and explosives taught him enough chemistry to pass a qualifying examination in college—a remarkable achievement, if we may trust Wylie's memory. Still, he obviously learned much more than his formal academic record shows.

The study of literature did interest Philip, particularly because by age fifteen he had definitely decided to be a writer. He recalled later that he grew up with the impression that all Wylies wrote and that he first saw the profession as profitable when, at age twelve, he received a dollar for a poem sold to the Presbyterian magazine, *The Continent*. In high school, he wrote a great deal, mostly verse, for various student publications. He specialized in parodies and imitations (among his favorite writers at the time were the poets, Vachel Lindsay and Alfred Noyes), showing exceptional skill in handling verse forms with complex rhyme schemes and other difficult technical requirements. His literary ambitions were apparently encouraged by his English teacher, George Harris, who frequently took his class to New York City to see plays and thus exposed Wylie to the glamour of the theater. By his senior year, he was visiting Greenwich Village on his own and dreaming of becoming a starving artist in an attic.

The activity outside of school which claimed his greatest enthusiasm was Scouting. Philip joined the Boy Scouts in 1915, and by 1919 he was a Boy Scout, First Class, with eighteen Merit Badges. One project required him to collect a sample of every kind of flora in the area; by the time he had completed the task, he had in effect given himself a good course in botany (all of his life he could identify thousands of trees and plants like a specialist) and had increased his love and respect for nature which had begun in rural Ohio. Philip also learned and put into practice the arts and skills of woodcraft, because the scoutmaster, Frederick K. Vreeland, an engineer and explorer, believed in training his charges to survive in a wilderness. Thus, the hiking and camping expeditions into the Adirondacks northwest of Lake George, New York, became major challenges to the courage, intelligence, and stamina of the boys. Wylie and a friend once treked fifty miles in a straight line to Mt. Marcy, not avoiding any obstacles and using their compass as a guide.

Philip did so well in woodcraft that Vreeland found him worthy of joining a small group on an exploring trip in the Canadian wilderness north of Kippewa in the summer of 1920. For nearly three months he helped to prepare maps and study the feeding habits of moose for the Smithsonian Institute; but, much more important, he also made a major discovery about animals. He often noted during his fact-gathering that certain animals seemed to have such human qualities as curiosity, a love of play, and even a sense of humor. Such traits were, according to Vreeland and other Behaviorists, imitations of human behavior. But this particular area, Wylie argued, had never been visited by any human being; the animals could not possibly be showing a learned behavior pattern. Was it possible that their "human" actions were inherent in their nature—in other words, "instinctive"? Vreeland, whose creed was that instincts do not exist and that all learning is done by trial and error, dismissed Wylie's observations as mere imagination. But Philip was certain about what he had seen; he knew that Behaviorism was wrong about animals and thus about the nature of human behavior as well. But not until he found Jung's writings fifteen years later was he able to counter the Behaviorists' thesis. Then in *Vipers, An Essay on Morals,* and, finally and most fully, in *The Magic Animal* he was able to make a definite contribution to man's knowledge about his own nature. But the process began in 1920 when he realized that, like himself, a moose came every day to a certain pond just to watch some half-grown beavers playing in the mud.

IV *College Days*

Wylie returned from the North Woods after classes had begun at Princeton but was allowed to register late in the fall of 1920. He was not destined to make an impressive academic record, for, as in high school, he applied himself only to the few subjects which interested him, and spent most of his time on extracurricular activities. His grades were so poor that he was suspended at the start of his fourth semester in 1922. During that term, a stint as a crewman on a freighter that sailed from Philadelphia to Vancouver gave him experiences which he later incorporated into his fiction. Readmitted in the fall, he did not noticeably improve in his classwork, and he was often openly contemptuous of the subject matter and methods of some of his teachers. One of them, Professor Root, who did not appreciate Wylie's unsolicited written opinion of an objective final examination in eighteenth century literature, gave him an "F" because of his "bad attitude." When Wylie protested to the dean that he had answered all of the questions correctly, the administrator refused to interfere, even though the grade meant the end of Wylie's college career.

He left the campus boiling with the anger against colleges, irrelevant curricula, pompous professors, and academic literary critics which later appeared in *Vipers* and many other works.[8] He also left filled with amazement that Root would react so violently to a completely justified criticism of his course. It never occurred to Wylie that he had been very sarcastic and absolutely tactless or that it is human nature to resent any criticism. In fact, this episode foreshadows many future ones when Wylie found himself astonished at how angry people became when he had done nothing but tell them the truth about themselves in the most cutting and satiric way imaginable. Such blind self-righteousness (which came, doubtless, from his being brought up in a minister's family) can obviously be an inconvenience to its owner, but without it Wylie would never have become a great satirist.

The college courses which eventually proved to be the most important in Wylie's development as a writer and thinker were those in physics, biology, and geology. He had not planned to take any of them but was forced to do so as the price of late admission by Dean McClenahan, a physics professor who believed that English majors should not be ignorant of science. Wylie's grades suggest that he did not overburden himself with information (he failed McClenahan's course twice and apparently acquired his impressive knowledge in private study after he left school), but he certainly understood the fundamental theories of these disciplines. More important, he grasped the implications of these concepts for modern man. Any remaining shreds of his belief in Presbyterianism vanished in Geology 305, a course in the theory of evolution taught by the elderly William B. Scott, the first disciple of Darwin in America. In fact, Wylie was exposed in all his science classes to the scientific method of discovering truth by experiment and objective observation and thus became persuaded that any belief in revealed religion was impossible.

At the same time, however, he began to reason that the scientific method might become the basis of a new religion if it were applied to the study of man himself, especially to his moral nature. This idea became one of the key ones in *Vipers* and occurred even earlier in his novels. Unfortunately, at that time there were no courses at Princeton—or anywhere else—devoted to modern psychology, which was considered "unscientific"; it was the custom of the Behaviorists to sneer at the mention of Freud. Yet, even as a freshman, Wylie, with typical independence of mind, began to read Freud's works. In them he discovered the principles on which he founded his own system: man is an animal, and he is governed by instincts, expecially sexual drive.

Although Wylie never completed the course of scientific study that McClenahan had planned, the dean's objective was achieved: a prospective writer had been made aware of the vast body of expanding knowledge that was reshaping man's world. In fact, Wylie became addicted to science and tried for the rest of his life to keep up with the latest developments through reading or conversations with the friends he made among scientists at the California Institute of Technology and elsewhere. Even his earliest books show his preoccupation with science, and by the 1930s he was condemning his fellow novelists for their smug and willful ignorance of physics, biology, and astronomy. He began increasingly to use his talents as a writer to explain the latest discoveries of science to the layman in understandable language. But not even his most optimistic teachers could have foreseen that he would someday develop into a "generalist" of such competence that he would become an advisor to the Congressional Committee on Atomic Energy and a respected panel member at conventions of scientists.

Wylie received his best grades in his literature courses because he wanted to learn from them how to be a writer. There were four in all, two surveys of English literature, one course in Shakespeare, and one in the work of eighteenth century authors. The latter introduced him to Jonathan Swift and Laurence Sterne, who became his literary idols. He admired the direct, clear style and the savage satire of Swift but was equally impressed with Sterne's love of experiment, indifference to literary convention, and determination to enjoy himself while writing exactly what he wished. The influence of both writers is seen in many of Wylie's books but most notably in the great *tour de force, Finnley Wren.* Wylie apparently did not encounter either American or modern writers in his college courses. For instance, he did not read Ralph Waldo Emerson or Henry David Thoreau until the mid-1930s. On his own, however, he explored the books of James Joyce, D. H. Lawrence, F. Scott Fitzgerald, Sinclair Lewis, and Aldous Huxley. It is not unexpected that one is reminded of these authors in early works like *Heavy Laden* and *Babes and Sucklings.*

While at Princeton, Wylie did a great deal of writing, all of it good practice but otherwise of little importance. He was a frequent contributor to the *Princetonian,* in which he signed his column, "Diogenes' Lamp," with the pun, Philip Speyce. He had also composed for that paper many poems which won him some local praise. His first book was a privately printed (three hundred copies) collection of these and other verses called *Dormitory Ditties* (1923), whose sale brought him a gratifying sum. His favorite writing project, however, was a successful hoax—a term paper about the works of a non-existent Victorian poet called Waterhouse which he illustrated with his own parodies of nineteenth century authors. The

professors who were fooled did not appreciate either the humor of
the situation or the skill of the young writer. To tell the truth, hardly anyone at Princeton shared his opinion of his potential, and it was
Professor Root who stated the consensus when he gleefully
declared, "You'll never even write a label for a soupcan." Philip
Wylie vowed that he would make him "eat" those words.

Another promise he made himself was that he would acquire a
great amount of money for himself. His stay at Princeton had
caused him to develop a life-long obsession with acquiring wealth.
His family had always lived in the genteel poverty common to those
in the ministry, but he had never felt inferior because of it until he
attended college and found himself humiliated by his peers who
were the sons of the well-to-do. On one occasion he was told that he
had been accepted for membership in the Cannon Eating
Club—but that he must first purchase a new suit in order to improve his appearance. He was unable to join because he did not
have enough money—and he could not in any case have afforded
the dues, as he discovered after he was taken into Key and Seal,
another fraternity.

Many similar embarrassments and slights were caused by his lack
of funds, but, even worse, Wylie began to desire the material
possessions, social position, and attractive female companions which
his "betters" had in such abundance. Like F. Scott Fitzgerald,
Wylie was therefore fated to be torn between his ambition to
become an artist and his obsession with those things which only
money can buy. Ten years later, when he was earning forty thousand dollars annually during the worst of the Depression, he noted
with satisfaction that many of his formerly high-living classmates
were now penniless. He could also say, with some justice, that his
remunerative hack work had made it possible for him to write books
like *Finnley Wren* for himself—that he was managing to have two
careers at once and was successful in both. Still, it is surprising to
find strongly materialistic aspirations in a writer who in books like
Vipers attacks the worldliness of American goals. Too, he might well
have been a greater writer if he had never gone to a school for the
rich and seen how pleasant their lives were.

CHAPTER 2

The Young Writer
(1923-1930)

WYLIE spent the next seven years trying to earn a living by writing. In his first two major ventures—in advertising and in staff work on a magazine—he was reasonably successful until circumstances forced him into what was to be his real career—that of a free-lancer. But even then the big income about which he dreamed continued to evade him.

I Advertising

Wylie began working in June, 1923, for Bernays and Thorson, a New York City public relations firm. He learned the art of ad writing quickly, grew ambitious, and, with the help of John Gordon Hamilton, a wealthy Princeton alumnus, established his own agency early in 1924. His later satiric comments on businessmen and their ethics came in part from his experiences at this time. Incidentally, Thornton in *Babes and Sucklings*, Stuyvesant Jones in *As They Reveled*, and the title character of *Finnley Wren* are public relations men.

Late in 1924, however, the little agency abruptly ceased to exist when a girl in Montclair, New Jersey, filed a suit charging Wylie with fathering her unborn child. The newspapers delightedly headlined the girl's account of a night of "hijinks in the manse" with the son of a prominent minister. Wylie had, in fact, had sexual intercourse with Henrietta "Toots" Hammond in the empty parsonage in the course of a "blind date" with her in the preceding August. But he was not the child's father: she had been several months pregnant when he met her, as was proved when the full-term child was born. At the trial, held on January 5, 1925, he was, nevertheless, declared to be the guilty party and required to support the infant. A later appeal reversed that decision, but the damage to Wylie was already done and irreparable.

Out of a job, deeply hurt by his father's refusal to appear with him in court (though he had arranged financing for the legal fees), and forced by public opinion to leave Montclair, his life apparently ruined, Wylie never forgot or forgave the injustice. He saw clearly that he had been punished solely because he had engaged in premarital sexual intercourse—a common, natural, and, he believed, harmless act that had no ethical significance; his only mistake lay in having it brought to public attention. He was, therefore, a victim of a middle-class community's self-righteous and hypocritical desire to prove its own alleged moral uprightness in sexual matters. Thus, it is not surprising that for the rest of his life Wylie almost obsessively campaigned for an honest examination of the nature of human sexual behavior and of the unsavory reasons for society's vicious treatment of "sexual offenders." He would certainly have written on the subject in any case, but not with the sustained anger that produced masterpieces like "A Specimen American Attitude" in *Vipers*. Nor, of course, would he have written *Finnley Wren*, whose hero suffers an identical persecution.

II *The* New Yorker *Staff Writer*

Looking for a job late in 1924, Wylie went to see Harold Ross, who was planning to publish a new magazine, the *New Yorker*. He got a position by promising to work without pay until he proved his worth. He was put on the payroll three months later and remained on the staff until March, 1927. Much of his time was spent in designing formats, pictorial layouts, and typography—an experience which he later put to good use in creating the unorthodox design of *Finnley Wren*. He wrote many unsigned items, such as contributions to "The Talk of the Town," and he published fifty-five signed poems, mostly light verse about the New York scene.

But far more important than his writing was his immersion in the whole New York literary scene of that era. Living in Greenwich Village and being a part of the bright young intellectual set surrounding Ross, he became acquainted with many of the most famous literary and artistic personalities in America, including Theodore Dreiser (their current idol), James Thurber, Claire Boothe Brokow, Alexander Woollcott, Dorothy Parker, Franklin P. Adams, and Heywood Broun. These people, along with their coterie of publishers, editors, and critics, constituted the heart of what Wylie would later call the "Liberal Intellectual Establishment." By temperament always a loner, not a joiner, Wylie saw them with the detachment of the outsider. He adjudged their sophistication to be shallow and imitative, their talent small but carefully promoted by their mutual admiration society, their knowledge of the real world distorted by their uncritical acceptance of Leftist theory and by their willful ignorance of science. Nearly every kind of modern art, music, and literature which they espoused seemed to him to be worthless: he could see no reason to praise James Joyce and Marcel Proust for being incomprehensible.[1]

But, in spite of Wylie's opinions of the members of the Establishment, he deeply desired to win their praise for the books he would someday write; he was certain that they would be able to recognize merit when they saw it. That day never came, and, years later, Wylie took his revenge by making the New York group the object of brilliant and cruel satire in *Finnley Wren* and in *The Smiling Corpse*. Eventually his feud with them found a basis besides his personal grievances, for in his later years he (perhaps correctly) blamed the members of the Liberal Intellectual Establishment for encouraging the most disastrous trends in American intellectual, political, and social life. The LIE was always his favorite villain, even more than Mom.

III *A New Direction*

Wylie was finally dropped from the *New Yorker* staff in the spring of 1927, an event that propelled him irrevocably into freelancing. Actually, ever since college he had been writing on his own—a try at a novel, a book on interior decoration, short stories. In fact, he had just completed a serious novel that he had submitted to Knopf. He obtained an agent, Miss Flora May Holly (then wellknown as the representative of Dreiser and Edna Ferber), and began to write for pulp magazines like *Black Mask, Zest,* and, all during 1929, *Live Girl Stories.* It was a precarious way to earn a living, so, starting in the fall of 1927, he worked for a year as advertising manager for Cosmopolitan Book Company during the day and wrote at night. He was never able to "break into" the quality magazines, however; in fact, the only significant short pieces from this period are the eleven "fables" which he placed in *Vanity Fair* from 1928 to 1930. These bits of fantasy were the forerunners of the amazing fables in *Finnley Wren* and *Opus 21* as well as of such novels of fantasy as *Gladiator, The Disappearance,* and *The Answer.*

One reason for Wylie's outpouring of pulp stories was Sally Ondeck, a former Powers model and divorcée whom he met in the spring of 1927 at a Greenwich Village party. They soon began living together and were married in April of the next year. Unfortunately for Wylie's literary aspirations, Sally's main object in life was money, and he knew that he could not hold her unless he provided it. A six-month stay in France in 1928, a winter vacation in Miami in 1929, the purchase of a house in East River, Connecticut—all are evidence of the vigor with which he pursued his goal. Little of Sally's true character emerges in the heroine of *Babes and Sucklings,* a fictional account of their year as free lovers in Greenwich Village; a much more accurate picture of her is given in *Finnley Wren.* By that time Sally had driven Wylie to alcoholism with her demands on his energy, her erratic behavior, and, most of all, her extraordinary indifference to marital fidelity.[2] But in 1927 Wylie still thought that he was a very lucky man.

IV   Heavy Laden

In the late spring of 1927, the firm of Alfred A. Knopf became the first to accept for publication a novel by Philip Wylie—an allegorical fantasy, *Titan.* However, the author wanted his first published novel to be a serious realistic work so that he would make a good impression on the critics. Therefore, he signed on May 7 a contract to write such a work; the new book, *Heavy Laden,* was completed rather quickly and issued in April, 1928. The novel is the story of Hugh McGreggor, who possesses the capacities necessary to be a great man but becomes only a good man. Handsome, athletic, intelligent, possessed of courage, human-kindness, and a strong will, he comes from generations of Scotch Presbyterians, whose system of ideas he accepts as his own and then attempts to impose on his own life, his family, and the modern world. Hugh's tragedy is not just that he is an anachronism or even that he drives his children from him: rather, it is that he despoils his own potential and in the end becomes a hypocrite, a *poseur,* a self-deceiver, and a fool—a man unable to perceive that he has fettered his own mind with an invalid system of belief and therefore can offer no valid solutions to the problems facing the young people of the twentieth century.

Actually, the novel is a barely fictionalized biography of the author's father and deals in detail with his first marriage, his heroism during a flood, his successful campaign to close the saloons in a Midwestern town, his second marriage and its tragic end (Wilmina Wylie had died in 1919 during minor surgery), his work as a chaplain in the Young Men's Christian Association during World War I, and his tenure as a prominent clergyman in New Jersey. Unifying the novel is the gradual and, finally, catastrophic disintegration of the father's relationship with his daughter, Ann, many of whose experiences are based on those of Philip Wylie.

McGreggor, according to the author, destroys both his intellectual integrity and his value to society by refusing to learn from the lessons of reality. He does not comprehend that his struggle to control the drinking habits of other people is only an attempt to display his own supposed moral superiority. He interprets the deaths of his wives as tests of his faith by God—not as evidence of the nonexistence of a deity. He praises God for giving his daughter, Ann, the strength to survive a burst appendix—not realizing that her recovery was brought about by the example of his courage and the toughness inherited from him. In France, he cannot comprehend why soldiers exposed to the meaningless horror and death of the trenches no longer have faith in the traditional conception of a benevolent God; he is of no help to young men who want to know what their lives are really all about.

Inevitably, after the war McGreggor has no patience with the younger generation, including Ann, that has grown up in a world in which science has exploded the bases for the old morality. Instead of helping them seek new answers, he insists on blind faith in God; and, by denying his sympathy and love to Ann, he drives her into rebellion and a life of dissolute behavior. Ever the egoist, and having learned nothing, at the end of the novel he interprets her denunciation of him and his beliefs as proof that he has failed to carry out his God-appointed mission. To punish himself, he gives up his comfortable tenure as a bland minister in a wealthy community for a miserable—and useless—self-exile in a Kansas town. (This episode is an instance of wishful thinking on Wylie's part. In real life, the Reverend Wylie moved on to a nationally known church.) In contrast to her father, Ann, who has rejected supernaturalism for an honest and intellectually valid view of life, marries one of her many lovers (a millionaire) and becomes the contented mother of three—triumphant proof of the rightness of her (and Wylie's) principles.

The structure of *Heavy Laden* reflects Wylie's determination that his reader share his evaluation of Hugh McGreggor. The book unfolds in sections of narrative interspersed with scenes of varying length (the final one is actually a playlet with stage directions); but Wylie, speaking in his own voice, accompanies every event with commentary and interpretation. He often brings the action to a complete halt with an extended address to the reader, and thus *Heavy Laden* seems at times more like a series of connected essays than a novel. The book would have been much more effective with fewer interruptions of the narrative and with a greater reliance on dialogue and action, rather than direct comment, to make its point.

Heavy Laden also suffers from the author's ambivalent attitude toward both Hugh and Ann. Wylie was not content to see only villainy in Hugh and to picture Ann as wholly admirable in her actions and character. Instead, he frequently reiterates the father's undeniable virtues and presents Ann's shortcomings without mercy ("a liar and a hypocrite, an embezzler from his pockets, a fallen woman, a drunkard, and a blasphemer"). Quite obviously, these evaluations show Wylie's frustrated love for his father and his own doubts and guilt feelings about his own actions, and, in theory, they should provide a much more valid picture of the consequences of the "generation gap" than a novel which eulogized the young. The trouble is that Wylie keeps changing sides, and the reader eventually grows weary of repeatedly changing *his* opinion; furthermore, the cumulative effect of Ann's various indiscretions is to erode his patience and sympathy; and, in the end, when she tries to destroy Hugh in front of a witness, the reader either sides with the father or decides that he has had enough of both of them. Since it was clearly Wylie's intention to close the book with Ann canonized by motherhood and as triumphant proof of the rightness of her principles, the book has failed.

One other very annoying aspect of *Heavy Laden* is the unclear writing. The narrative and dialogue are usually unblemished, but key sentences in the author's commentary, especially when Wylie is pontificating, are often unintelligible; and, since the author relies so heavily on direct statement, the reader soon becomes confused and irritated. Like many young writers, Wylie was too fond of polysyllabic words and impressive-sounding aphorisms; he really needed a dictionary and an unsympathetic editor along with a lot of writing experience.

Elsewhere the style shows signs of real promise. There are some obvious clichés and sporadic overwriting, but there are few of those unusual words which he had acquired from his father's vocabulary-building exercises and which he in later books often used excessively. Wylie on occasion demonstrates a good ear for dialogue; he is at his best in the passages where the minister is delivering a sermon or is discussing religion in ritualistic language that has lost its meaning. Yet, despite the at least acceptable level of competence in most of the dialogue, many of the long set speeches in which the characters present their views of life are stilted and unreal. The worst occur in the final confrontation of Ann and Hugh, the scene in which all of Wylie's skills abandoned him.

Heavy Laden, in addition to its other weaknesses, shows the influence of all the young writer's favorite authors. The wild life of the Fast Set seems to be modeled on Fitzgerald's accounts. Hemingway's *The Sun Also Rises* occupies a place of honor in Ann's apartment, and certain descriptive passages imitate his famous style. Wylie later admitted to having been influenced by Sinclair Lewis and Ben Hecht. Throughout the book, of course, is the pervasive effect of Aldous Huxley and his endlessly talking purveyors of the latest anti-establishment ideas.

But, in spite of these influences, the authentic attitudes of Wylie emerge in passages which clearly foreshadow *Finnley Wren* as well as other novels. One is his sense of the black comedy implicit in life: one of the passengers on a train approaching a flood-weakened bridge is a lovelorn young man saying to himself, "I wish I could die." Another is his obsession with the horror of physical pain and mutilation, often summed up in a simple sentence: "The man who lay in his entrails lapsed into silence." We also find a Swiftian preoccupation with the less esthetically pleasing body functions, as well as the misanthropy which seems to grow from this distaste. The latter is particularly evident in the five short essays addressed to the reader.

In the first, he describes mankind's unsavory nature and then declares, "I hate your guts." In the second, he condemns the reader's prurient interest in the characters' sex lives, which he has just been describing in titillating terms. In the third, he defends his use of wickedness and sacrilege with *ad hominem* attacks on his alleged critics. Elsewhere, he presents several cynical aphorisms in the hope that they will do "profound harm" to the reader but with the "confidence that only the meaning of my words will elude you, the sense being obvious." These outbursts of outrage, adorned with scorn, mockery, derision, jeers, outright contempt, and insult are, in form, content, and tone, a fair warning of what would explode in both *Finnley Wren* and, most astoundingly, in *Generation of Vipers*.

Although *Heavy Laden* received lavish praise from Theodore Dreiser, who wrote the advertisements for Knopf, it sold only 6,579 copies, earning the author a small reputation and less money. Perhaps more important was the fact that at least some of his antagonism toward his father had been given an outlet; at least, in the future his portraits of fathers would not be recognizable as Reverend Wylie. He was, in fact, following a familiar pattern: most beginning novelists write their first books about the trauma of their own upbringing. With that matter concluded, he was ready to move on to themes of more universal application.

V Babes and Sucklings

Wylie's second novel, *Babes and Sucklings*, published by Knopf in April, 1929, explores the subject to which he would return in much of his later work—the complexities of the relationship between men and women in the modern world. In an attempt to show the "intricate and imponderable . . . course two intelligent persons must follow in this muddled era in order to attain and continue the attitude of love towards each other," Wylie tells the story of two years in the lives of Cynthia Sherman and Thornton (his other name is never given), and he carefully analyzes their attitudes and motives as their relationship evolves.

When Cynthia meets Thornton at a party in Greenwich Village, she has just arrived from California after an unsatisfying marriage to a dull and unappreciative man; she hopes to find a more stimulating existence among the wealthy, intelligent, and sophisticated of New York City. Thornton is an unattached bachelor possessed of charm, wit, sensitivity, and real potential as a writer. These young people are immediately strongly attracted to each other, consummate the relationship within forty-eight hours, and in a few weeks are living together very happily, "in harmony and fidelity, as settled and organized as two Babbitts." They are bound by their mutual love and not by religious, social, or legal ties; their strong emotional attachment sustains their relationship even after a quarrel when he hits her in a drunken jealous rage. By dint of their intelligent efforts to gain knowledge of each other and by the practice of restraint and care, they adjust to each other's personalities and avoid or surmount the inevitable clashes and crises.

Two of their acquaintances, Don Shaw and Geraldine McGrath, engage in a more conventional courtship, during which she pretends to be physically attracted to him, and then a most familiar kind of marriage—one in which a frigid and materialistic wife, exploiting the husband's conception of marital ties as permanent, denies him her sexual favors and uses matrimony as a way of accumulating money without effort on her part. Trapped in a bad marriage, Don accepts a life of continence, and, intimidated by Gerry's nagging and making of "scenes," he engages in the unethical business practices necessary to their economic advancement.

In the meantime, the unconventional union of Cynthia and Thornton encounters difficulties which erode their feelings for each other. A major problem comes from Thornton's frustrations in trying to earn a living: he wants to write a novel of literary merit; instead, he can barely meet their expenses with the countless potboilers on which he spends all his time and energy. The death of Michael Paladini, Thornton's best friend, deprives him of the emotional support and advice which he needs. Then Cynthia becomes pregnant, increasing their financial difficulties; her frequent periods of illness add to the constant strain on their nerves. By the time the child is born dead, Cynthia can no longer bear the grim atmosphere and their endless misunderstandings; she resolves to leave him and become the mistress of wealthy Murray Dean, whose unsolicited gifts and attention have contributed to her growing dissatisfaction with her life. After a few days of separation, she discovers that she still cares for Thornton, and the couple is again united, this time in marriage.

Babes and Sucklings is one of Wylie's most convincing pictures of human relationships because it contains few overtly dramatic events but concentrates instead on scenes involving subtle changes of attitude or mood, small discoveries and decisions, moments of communication or alienation. For instance, during Cynthia's first visit to Thornton's apartment, when she is strangely moved by his singing of a ballad about a lonely cowboy, it becomes obvious to the reader—though not to Cynthia—that she has fallen in love. Wylie is even more skillful in capturing nuances of feeling in his account of the next day, when the two of them start "celebrating" Thornton's loss of his job with drinks before lunch, spend the afternoon in a pleasantly incoherent daze, and by night are peacefully asleep in the same bed.

Similarly, a quarrel that takes place months later suggests a different kind of intimacy—one born of disillusionment—when Cynthia says, "Are you going to be that way all day? Because if you are, I'm going out." Wylie might well have produced a masterpiece of realism if he had allowed the relationship to continue to disintegrate under the strain of real-life pressures. Instead, he introduces Murray Dean's schemes to undermine Cynthia's morale, and, with these wholly unnecessary and far-fetched machinations, he destroys the illusion of truth which he had carefully created.

Wylie again drew heavily from his own experiences when he composed *Babes and Sucklings*—a fact which partly explains how he was able to set down an eighty-thousand-word novel during the ten-day voyage home from his honeymoon in France. Although Wylie quite correctly asserted that the book is not an autobiography, the central situation is obviously modeled after his own pre-marital union with Sally—and especially the problems that arose from his drinking, her tendencies toward infidelity, her pregnancy and miscarriage, and the harrowing tensions caused by his writing.

Thornton, the free-lancer and free-lover, is clearly based on the author, but he is an immature version of Wylie, cynical about the world and hating its hypocrisy but protected from despair by his surviving illusions and dreams. Michael, on the other hand, is the man Wylie secretly feared he might become—an idealist driven nearly mad by his knowledge that the self-righteous world would never change, for a while taking out his frustrations on fools and hypocrites in Rabelaisian invective, but, in the end, turning his fury inward upon himself until only death could bring him release from his pain.

In a slightly different way, Sally inspired Wylie's portraits of both Cynthia and Gerry. To an objective observer of Sally Wylie's behavior, there would seem to be little resemblance between her and the predominantly virtuous heroine of the novel. But Wylie, of course, was not a detached spectator of his own marital life, and his portrait of Cynthia represents his misguided and chivalrous conception of Sally as a woman with understandable feminine weaknesses but with nothing unprincipled in her makeup. On the other hand, in a part of his mind he must have been fully aware of her true nature: it cannot be mere coincidence that Gerry's character and actions correspond almost exactly with those of Sally Wylie, who differs from her only in having a higher degree of intelligence and greater shrewdness in dealing with men.

One unfortunate consequence of Wylie's muddled thinking about his real-life sources is, naturally, that the central theme of *Babes and Sucklings* is never clearly presented. Crucial passages in his authorial commentaries are often either frustratingly ambiguous or beyond comprehension—a sure indication that Wylie did not know what he meant. The reader may also find that sometimes the author's analyses are not really correct interpretations of the actions that precede them or that the writer may even contradict himself in later passages. Not even the characters who serve as Wylie's spokesmen can be relied on for clarity, accuracy, or consistency. As a result, for example, we may read nearly half the novel before discovering that it is not a defense of "companionate marriage," as it at first appears to be. There can be little doubt that the author was, in effect, groping his way toward the meaning of his narrative. The thesis which finally emerges from the confusion (and, in retrospect, gives a semblance of unity to the novel) is that any relationship between a man and a woman can be a success only if the partners are capable of truly loving each other.

Wylie's flawed handling of his theme is overshadowed by his remarkable achievements in character portrayal. Each of his major figures is a completely believable and complex human being who displays a variety of traits, some of them contradictory, as in real life, and these people undergo changes in personality in response to new situations and problems. Even the minor ones, with the exception of the stereotyped Murray Dean, are given qualities that individualize them and make them credible. Wylie's methods of revealing character represent a significant advance over those in *Heavy Laden*, especially in his increased use of a person's words and thoughts to delineate him. Thus, the character's choice of subject, his opinions, the diction and rhythms of his speech, and even the sound of his voice reinforce and enlarge upon the reader's initial impression of him.

The portrait of Thornton is the best example of Wylie's ability to show change in a character—or, rather, to trace the process by which certain qualities already present become prominent in altered circumstances. In the opening chapters, the young man displays the sophistication, self-sufficiency, cheerful cynicism, and enthusiasm for living we would expect to find in a member of New York's "Smart Set." Soon, however, we become aware that Thornton is, to a degree, playing a role. Love and suffering have not yet revealed and shaped his true character.

Consequently, one major effect of his relationship with Cynthia is to bring out previously unsuspected qualities—especially his weaknesses. His brash self-confidence gradually gives way to self-doubt that nearly immobilizes him. His frustrations expose in him a nasty streak of violence that he turns against others and then himself, as in his self-destructive drinking when Cynthia abandons him. His best traits—his sensitivity, his idealism, his hopeful-ness—are still apparent—but they only increase his vulnerability and undermine his will to endure. Wylie's picture of the decay of Thornton's personality under stress is painfully real and is so con-vincing that we close the book a little ashamed of having witnessed the humiliation of a fellow human being.

The portrait of Cynthia is solid evidence of Wylie's already matured skill in that most difficult of all areas in writing—the crea-tion of believable women characters who are neither peerless ex-amples of virtue nor demons of unfathomable evil. Her attractive qualities are her honesty about her emotions, her disdain for hypocrisy, her tolerance, intelligence, and warmth, her almost maternal ability to fall in love with Thornton's boyishness. Nevertheless, she is as flawed as he, for she is fundamentally very selfish and, like most contemporary women, is conditioned by her culture to place material goals ahead of all others and to regard any male as expendable if he fails to satisfy her needs or desires. Although Wylie praises her for her efforts to avoid being like most modern women, it is precisely when she stops making those efforts that Thornton's real troubles begin. Her illness is partly to blame, as is Thornton's inability to surmount his difficulties; but the male reader can never forget that she walked out of one marriage or really forgive her for her cold-blooded contemplation of a loveless but remunerative sexual relationship with Murray Dean. This dis-passionate view of sex as a commodity is, Wylie says, a woman's most frightening quality.

In portraying Geraldine McGrath, Wylie set out to create a character who would be the epitome of all the qualities which he detested in the modern American woman. He was eminently successful, for Gerry reveals through her actions and words such at-tributes as laziness, an insatiable greed for material possessions, and a complete absence of sexual feelings—all the while defending her life style with blatant hypocrisy and smug self-righteousness. She is immediately recognizable because her real-life prototypes are depressingly common, and she is made even more believable by Wylie's analysis of the causes of her deficiencies. She is the product of a culture that indoctrinates women with the idea that sex is degrading and unpleasant for the female. It also teaches that a woman has the right to expect men to provide for her material desires; her weapon and tool in the war between the sexes is her body: coitus and the promise of it are to be used, without qualms, to achieve her goals.

Gerry therefore has no inkling that her frigidity is unnatural or that her inability to find fulfillment in sex has doomed her to a restless search for a substitute—money and possessions, which, her society tells her, guarantee happiness. But she is more than a type character or a case study in a psychology text: she is also sharply in-dividualized by certain qualities that are all her own. She compels belief in a way not equalled until Wylie described Helen Holbein in *Finnley Wren*, and we hate Gerry as if she were real.

Despite the speed of composition, the style of *Babes and Sucklings* is a major improvement over that of *Heavy Laden*. As already noted, certain passages of commentary by Wylie (and oc-casionally by a philosophically inclined character) defy paraphrase; but otherwise the novel is a model of clear and effective prose that is also a pleasure to read. There are no examples of "purple" overwriting and just a few inappropriate words like "matutinal." The dialogue, in general, sounds like that of real people; moreover, it frequently reflects the personality and educational level of the in-dividual speaker. Several of Thornton's drunken ramblings, which continue for pages at a time, are wildly funny as well as a perfect evocation of an inebriated mind. Both he and Michael specialize in monologues in which they can display their delight in rhetorical flourishes and command of the idiom. The best of these *tours de force* are the equal of Wylie's tirades in *Vipers*—truly an astonishing performance from such a young and inexperienced writer.

Long out of print, *Babes and Sucklings* was re-issued in 1966 as a paperback entitled *The Party*. The reappearance was long overdue, for, if this novel is not one of his best, it often comes close. Its in-sights into human psychology, the three exceptional pieces of characterization, the sophisticated handling of scenes and dialogue, and the grasp of the complexity of man-woman relationships cannot be casually dismissed. At the very least, it offers a preview of the kind of subjects and the writing skills which would make *Finnley Wren* a classic.

VI   Gladiator

Knopf published Wylie's third novel, *Gladiator*, in March, 1930. It was, in fact, a completely re-written version of "Titan," which had been accepted for publication three years earlier. Some of the delay may have resulted from Wylie's unwillingness to make the changes demanded by Knopf. The original, written in his *New Yorker* period, had been strongly influenced by his admiration for the eccentric English master, Laurence Sterne. He recalled (taped interview with Keefer, August, 1966), "I had a little preface to each chapter—there were twenty chapters, and each chapter began with a different letter of the alphabet. I was having a little fun like that, playing anagrams and things, but Knopf made me re-write it as a straight unobstructed narrative. That's all, and I didn't want to do that. I wanted to be an eighteenth century kind of writer."

Wylie finally surrendered to the publisher's demands, but, when *Gladiator* sold only 2,568 copies, he terminated his contract with Knopf on the convenient grounds that the novel had not been given adequate promotion. The real reason for his action was that he needed a publisher who would be sympathetic towards his literary ideals. He was right, of course: Knopf would automatically have rejected *Finnley Wren*.

In actuality, the deletions did not prevent Wylie from carrying out his primary purpose, which was to present a serious theme: his belief that, when a truly superior person tries to win acceptance and put his talents to use in the world, he will be frustrated and defeated by mankind's stupidity, pettiness, jealousy, unenlightened self-interest, and indifference to moral principles. As often in his books, Wylie was expressing a conviction based on his own experiences. As he said in the above-mentioned interview, "I was a young man thinking I was pretty wonderful, and I could not find a place to fit in the world."

Accordingly, he gave his hero, Hugo Danner, his own qualities—intelligence, sensitivity, idealism, moral earnestness—and added innocence about the world he was to encounter. But a significant difference exists between the two people; unlike Wylie, Hugo possesses supernatural physical strength and a nearly invulnerable body. Although it is tempting to see the invention of this super man as an act of ego projection or adolescent wish-fulfillment, it was really an instance of the workings of the same wildly creative imagination that would also produce in later years an invisible man, an angel from outer space, beast-men for horror movies, a man from Mars, and a giant a thousand miles high. Still, having a hero like Hugo served a very practical purpose in that it enabled Wylie to give the ultimate illustration of his theme: even the most gifted and powerful man who ever lived cannot alter human history or cope with mankind's intrinsic baseness.

The story of Hugo Danner is the chronicle of a journey from innocent idealism through humiliations to final disillusionment and despair. The son of an obscure college biology teacher, Hugo is born with a body of incredible sturdiness and strength, the result of his father's discovery of a "plasma" that alters the nature of tissue. He is taught self-control and is instilled with a sense of obligation to use his strength only for good. At college, he excels in athletics, but leaves school after accidentally killing an opposing football player. When World War I begins, he joins the French army because he believes that, in the struggle to save civilization, he has at last found a worthy cause.

But the convention-bound military has no place for Hugo except in the trenches as an ordinary rifleman. In the post-war era, he tries in vain to find in America an uncorrupted statesman whom he can support in efforts to stop another war. Later, his plan to rescue two radicals unjustly sentenced to death is thwarted by their fellow Communists, who are scheming to use them as martyrs. He finds that capitalists are equally indifferent to human life: when he saves a clerk trapped in a burglar-proof bank vault, he is arrested as a menace to property. Ordinary workingmen are also basely materialistic, as he discovers when his own union insists that he be fired because he works too hard and endangers their jobs. Finally, Hugo reveals his dilemma to a noted archeologist, a man dedicated to reason, the scientific method, and the search for truth. His proposal—that Hugo create a race of titans with sufficient power to control and, if necessary, destroy mankind—at first appeals to him. But he soon rejects it, preferring to leave the world unchanged rather than destroy it. The titans, after all, would still be human beings, and to entrust them with limitless power would be to invite certain disaster. Alone on a mountain top, Hugo prays for release from his fruitless life and is mercifully answered by a lightning bolt.

The portrait of Hugo Danner is given additional human dimensions by the account of his love life, which is as unsuccessful as his other efforts. Like any other man, he wants a woman who will be his lover, friend, and companion; but, because he is different from others, he is condemned to a nearly unbearable isolation and loneliness. He dreams of finding warmth and kindness but, like most of Wylie's heroes, encounters no female with those qualities. His first sweetheart has only marriage as her goal; the college girls he admires are inaccessible because they are not interested in a man without money; Iris, the first "liberated" self-willed modern girl in Wylie's books, uses him to satisfy her ego; his first mistress, Charlotte, is an ignorant lower-class girl unworthy of him. His failure illustrates one of Wylie's favorite themes: the vast majority of women are so selfish, greedy, cruel, and insensitive that no man, and particularly not the truly superior one, can hope to find the love he needs. Defeated by the nature of the female, his pathetic needs unsatisfied, Hugo may well be Everyman.

One of the main challenges to Wylie in writing *Gladiator* was the need to devise spectacular feats for Hugo to perform and then to make them seem probable. Our exposure to the Superman comic strip unfortunately obscures the originality of many of these inventions, which, according to Wylie, as well as recent scholars,[3] were "borrowed" from *Gladiator*. Hugo hurtling across a river in a single leap, bounding fifty feet straight up in the air, holding a cannon above his head with one arm, killing a shark by ripping its jaws apart with his bare hands, felling a charging bull with a fist between the eyes, lifting an automobile by its bumper and turning it around in the road—all of these were, in 1930, fresh and new and very exciting to read about.

Wylie solves the problem of making these feats believable in two ways. First, he asserts that Hugo's strength is not supernatural but is an application of the same principles of nature which give insects like the ants the ability to handle great loads. Second, he places reasonable limits on what his hero can do. For example, Hugo has to eat tremendous amounts of food to produce his energy; he suffers excessively from hunger and thirst; and once, after killing a thousand Germans in their trenches, he faints from exhaustion. He never lifts more than four tons at a time, and, as an infant, he was a week old before he could lift himself with one arm. Furthermore, most of the time he acts as normal as possible to conceal his strength from the world.

With the exception of *Finnley Wren, Gladiator* is stylistically as good as anything Wylie was to write in the next fifteen years. The prose is clear, simple, easy to follow, without awkwardness or obscurity (except in a half dozen widely scattered sentences), and quite effective in passages delineating physical action. At times, he uses trite expressions, but these, too, are relatively few, perhaps because of the work of a good editor. There is a great deal of profanity and vulgarity in the dialogue, all of it appropriate to the speaker and situation, of course, but a bit unusual for a novel of the time. Missing are the unusual "big" words so common in Wylie's later writing, although there are a few "purple passages" of pompous prose. The handling of dialogue is satisfactory: no one's speech ever sounds stilted or unnatural, but, on the other hand, few lines ever sharply individualize the character or suggest his tone of voice.

VII   Blondy's Boy Friend

The fourth book of Wylie's apprentice period, *Blondy's Boy Friend,* was issued in May, 1930, by Chelsea House, an affiliate of Smith and Street, the pulp fiction syndicate. This fifty-thousand-word novelette centers on Irene Blaine, who falls in love with a young doctor and then has to prove him innocent of a homicide. The book was published under the pseudonym, Leatrice Homesley, because Wylie considered it little more than pulp fiction and wanted to conceal his authorship in order to protect his public image as a "literary" man. In fact, *Blondy's Boy Friend* has never appeared in any list of Wylie's novels.

The book is, nevertheless, a significant sample of Wylie's commercial writing during his period of literary apprenticeship, and it reveals one important fact: Wylie, with three very promising "serious" novels to his credit, was still virtually an amateur at popular fiction and seemed to have no talent whatsoever for producing it. His handling of the traditional elements of a murder mystery plot, at which he would later become a master in the pages of *American Magazine,* is imitative and inept; we might even mistake the final scene, in which the murderers are exposed, for a parody. In presenting the love story, Wylie manages to repeat all the clichés of that genre, but there are isolated moments when he evokes the poignancy of romantic yearnings in a manner that foreshadows his accomplishments in *The Footprint of Cinderella, Return of a Prodigal, Second Honeymoon,* and parts of *Finnley Wren.*

The real significance of *Blondy's Boy Friend* in Wylie's development as a commercial writer lies in his choice of a heroine and in his technique for revealing her character. Irene is the first of a long line of "Wylie girls"—irreverent, self-reliant, free-spirited, determinedly modern creatures whose brash behavior and fondness for contemporary slang belie their susceptibility to "falling hard" and permanently for the "right man." This type, in endless variation, proved to be irresistibly attractive to readers of both sexes in the 1930s. But the secret of Irene's appeal (and that of many of her successors) is that Wylie, using the same sophisticated devices he had perfected for "literary" novels, enables the reader to see the appealingly human woman inside the hard-boiled cynic. Obviously, what Wylie needed most at this time was some good professional advice about how to put creations like her into saleable stories.

CHAPTER 3

The Early 1930s
(1930-1934)

B ETWEEN the publication of *Blondy's Boy Friend* in 1930
and *Finnley Wren* in 1934, Wylie suddenly became a financial
success. In that period, he sold about forty articles and stories to the
"slick" magazines, made money from most of the eight novels he
wrote, and had a remunerative role in the making of at least five
motion pictures. The quality of this vast outpouring is extremely
uneven, but his "commercial" fiction was good enough to enable
him at last to win recognition from the most influential magazine
editors of the period. In any case, these "entertainments" (as
Graham Greene called his own lighter works) were, as Wylie later
said, good practice for the better books he would eventually
produce, and we often find in them, sometimes quite directly
stated, the iconoclastic ideas that would later make him famous.

The cause of this spectacular improvement in Wylie's fortunes
occurred in the spring of 1930. In rapid succession, he became
professionally and personally involved with the four men who, each
in his own way, almost overnight turned a nearly unknown young
writer into one of America's best-paid free-lance authors and, less
obviously, made possible his more important other career in both
"literary" fiction and social satire. These men were Edwin Balmec,
Harold Ober, John Farrar, and Stanley Rinehart.

Wylie became acquainted with Balmer, the editor of *Redbook*,
because of a quarrel with his agent, Flora May Holly. The incident
occurred during a conference about her failure to sell any of his
stories to the quality periodicals. To resolve the impasse, Wylie
proposed that she pay a personal visit to Balmer's office on his
behalf. She refused and said that she was afraid of the man; but
Wylie became angry because he regarded her explanation as an ex-
cuse for either incompetence or indifference. He immediately went

to see Balmer by himself. The two men became friendly at once, and the editor began to suggest plots for stories. Afterwards, Wylie, determined to prove his merits, wrote that night a story based on one of Balmer's ideas and took it to him the next day. The editor was, naturally, astounded at Wylie's speed, and, more important, liked the piece and bought it for four hundred dollars. That sale was to be only the first of many to *Redbook*, which eventually printed even more of his work than the *Saturday Evening Post*.

Wylie's visit also marked the start of an unusual and mutually profitable collaboration. Balmer had a genius for inventing plots and was already well-known for his highly imaginative fiction; but he was a busy editor and, moreover, disliked the drudgery of composition. Wylie, by contrast, had been having trouble devising the strong story-lines which are the chief ingredient in magazine fiction; but he could fill in the mere outline of a story with phenomenal ease and speed, and in a craftsmanlike manner. Therefore, during the next four or five years, they repeatedly pooled their complementary talents.

A majority of Wylie's early stories and short novels for *Redbook* were based on "concepts" suggested by Balmer—in effect, commissioned by him as a part of his search for good material for the magazine. The two men, working together in the same way, also produced five very profitable novels which appeared in other periodicals and as books under both their names, again with Wylie doing most of the writing, though this time getting credit only as the co-author. These joint enterprises virtually ceased after 1935 because the protégé had learned from the master all he needed to know and, partly through him, had made a reputation for himself. They remained on good terms, and Balmer continued to take a personal interest in the younger man's career. In fact, it was he who nominated him in *Redbook* as "the successor to F. Scott Fitzgerald" and who actively encouraged him to write increasingly serious fiction for the magazine in the late 1930s.

After dismissing Miss Holly, Wylie allied himself with a much more promising agent, Harold Ober. His choice was excellent. The fifty-year-old Ober had had years of experience in his business, was well-known as Fitzgerald's representative, and had just founded his own firm. Like Balmer, he recognized Wylie's potential and dedicated himself to his cause. Within a few months, Ober had brought Wylie to the attention of George Lorimer of the *Saturday*

Evening Post; the story, "Darkness," and an article, "Why Colleges Fail Students," were printed in the prestigious *Post* in the fall. This major breakthrough was followed by sales to *Collier's Weekly* and *Liberty,* and, in just a few years, to *American, Harper's, Cosmopolitan,* and practically every periodical in the country—and all of these sales were accomplished during the darkest days of the Great Depression, when well-known, established writers could not sell a word.

Ober, in addition to being an expert in the techniques of marketing, also served his client as a shrewd literary advisor, reading his torrents of manuscripts, suggesting changes that would improve a story's chances, rejecting in advance material which he knew was unsaleable. The services of his firm included even the correcting and retyping of Wylie's original drafts, leaving him free to spend his time on writing. The two men remained close friends and business associates until Ober's death, even though other firms offered Wylie more favorable financial deals after he became famous. In fact, he, with characteristic loyalty, stayed with the firm even after Ober was gone.

In 1930, Wylie also found the kind of book publisher he needed—Farrar and Rinehart. He had first met John Farrar, then an editor at *Bookman,* in 1921 or 1922, when Wylie took him some of the poetry he was writing at Princeton. Farrar had, even at that time, encouraged him to pursue a career in literature; and, when he and Stanley Rinehart established their own firm in 1929, he urged Wylie to let them publish his books. Eventually Wylie agreed and terminated his frustrating relationship with Knopf—amid, incidentally, mutual recriminations. But everything went well in his affiliation with Farrar and Rinehart for the next thirty-one years. They rarely interfered with his freedom as an artist or thinker; they always worked hard to sell his books; and they were willing to risk their money on unconventional works like *Finnley Wren* and *Vipers.* Wylie, in turn, produced not only the great books which lent prestige to Farrar and Rinehart but also a constant outpouring of lesser works that made him one of their most reliable money earners. In short, on the friendship and support of these men was built the success of Wylie's most productive years. He remained with Farrar and Rinehart until the early 1960s, when they finally gave up control of the firm and the new management began rejecting his books.

I   The Murderer Invisible

The Murderer Invisible, Wylie's first novel for Farrar and Rinehart and the best of the eight which appeared in the early 1930s, was issued in January, 1931. Originally entitled *The Invisible Man,* the book had been composed in 1930, when Wylie was trying to break his contract with Knopf; the strategy of changing its name to *The Murderer Invisible* enabled him to avoid legal entanglements. As the initial title acknowledged, he had borrowed from H. G. Wells' classic story of 1897 the basic premise—that it is possible to make an object completely transparent. On it he built his own story; he set it in contemporary New Jersey and New York City and invented a plot full of exciting events and cliff-hanger suspense.

The theme of the story—that human beings, not being godlike, cannot be trusted with the power of gods—is also Wylie's. He had used it once before, in the closing pages of *Gladiator,* when Hugo Danner chooses not to use that power and to take the secret of his strength to the grave. In his new book, Wylie demonstrates how correct Danner's decision had been by showing what happens when another superman, the possessor of the greatest scientific brain in the world, elects, instead, to use whatever force is necessary to impose his vision of Utopia on his fellow man.

The title character of *The Murderer Invisible* is William Carpenter, a genius the equal of Einstein. Rejected by women because of his physical ugliness, ostracized by his fellow men, who resent his superiority of intellect, and cheated of his fortune by trusted business associates, the former idealist has become a bitter recluse. After fifteen years of research, he develops a chemical compound that can make him invisible and thus powerful enough to avenge himself on his enemies and to seize control of America from "the stupid masses"; he plans to put the government in the hands of "an autocracy of science" who will bring about Carpenter's lifelong dream of a new social order free of war, greed, poverty, and superstition.

The only people who know about Carpenter's discoveries are Bromwell Baxter, who had helped him in his research, and his niece, Daryl Carpenter, with whom the older scientist has fallen in love. They are unable to stop him as he murders the men who cheated him, robs banks to replenish his funds, and then undertakes a campaign of "constructive terrorism" by exploding bombs that cut off the water, power, and telephone services of New York City.

He then calls upon the nation to accept him as dictator and savior. When the United States government refuses to surrender, he blows up the Capitol itself and then annihilates Grand Central Station at the rush hour. The nation continues to resist, but no precautions are effective against Carpenter because no one is trying to locate an invisible man—at least until Baxter persuades the President of the truth. But, in the end, Daryl is the one who destroys him, by acting as bait and then by making him visible to his pursuers by splashing ink on him.

The change of Carpenter from idealist to monster illustrates a thesis that would be central to *Vipers*—the person who is not aware of the laws that govern his inner nature is condemned to be a slave and victim of it. Carpenter, trained only in the physical sciences and without knowledge of psychology, does not realize that the decisions made by his giant intellect are really governed by his emotions, particularly his unsatisfied yearnings for love, acclaim, and all the other manifestations of acceptance. Had he been aware of his compulsions, he might have controlled them and spared mankind much sorrow and himself his own moral decay and untimely death. Self-awareness would also have led to knowledge of others and prepared him for the fact that no amount of force can make people give up their cherished and misguided beliefs, for which they ignorantly choose to die. Furthermore, unlocked from the prison of his own ego, he would have been able to identify with others and thus would have been incapable of causing human suffering, no matter how good his cause might be.

Wylie also intended his story to show the danger of power in the hands of an intellectual because, like Nathaniel Hawthorne, he believed that a man dominated by his intellect and without the restraining influence of the heart or of a profoundly ethical nature cannot be trusted with control over his fellows, whom he regards as abstractions and not as flesh and blood entities. A good example of what can happen in such a case was, in fact, already taking place in Soviet Russia, where millions had died as the direct result of the cold-blooded decisions made by Lenin, Trotsky, and their successors.

Wylie definitely had the Red idealogues in mind when he created Carpenter, for in the story a "radical novelist" (in other words, a Communist) named Sanderling voices his approval of the invisible man's plan to remake society (a scheme which includes the abolition of marriage, churches, political parties, and private property), and he sees nothing wrong with "the destruction of the rabble" necessary to achieve those ends. This kind of advocacy of limitless savagery in the name of a nineteenth century intellectual's impossible dream of a "scientifically" ordered society was all too familiar to Wylie, who had, of course, heard it endlessly mouthed by the members of the Liberal Intellectual Establishment.

Wylie also tried to show the error in the notion that "scientists" (as distinguished from others with powerful minds) are well suited to be leaders of men. Basing his evaluation on his personal knowledge of many brilliant researchers in the physical sciences, he declared that they were, in reality, very poorly equipped for such a task. Narrowly trained in their speciality, never exposed to any of the humanities, isolated in their laboratories, arrogantly believing the myth that they were superior to their fellows, and ignorant of what a study of psychology might have told them about themselves, they were, in truth, a menace to mankind. Wylie would not realize for nearly fifteen years how right he had been in this opinion, and by then the nuclear researchers—without the least sense of moral responsibility—would have used their discoveries in "pure" science to arm the world with super bombs.[1]

In addition to the thought-provoking themes, many other elements in *The Murderer Invisible* earn it a high place among Wylie's works. Individual scenes, such as the one in which Carpenter, invisible except for his skeleton, is pursued by a lynch mob through an empty amusement park, illustrate the awesome fertility of the author's imagination. The portrayal of Carpenter, who is not a stereotyped "mad scientist" but a complex mixture of good and evil, compares favorably with Wylie's earlier attempts to reveal character through in-depth psychological analysis. In fact, Wylie is so successful that the reader never entirely loses sympathy for the villain; and, in the end, when Carpenter is betrayed by his desperate need to believe that he has found a woman who loves him, the reader finds it difficult not to identify with him instead of with those who have brought him to justice. Probably the most impressive aspect of the novel is, however, the air of verisimilitude which Wylie gave to even the most improbable of events, usually by surrounding them with realistic detail in lifelike settings. He was, in fact, very proud of the ingenious way in which he had made an impossible feat—the achieving of complete invisibility—seem entirely plausible. Not even the great H. G. Wells, he noted, had been able to accomplish that goal.

The Murderer Invisible enjoyed some currency, selling nearly seven thousand copies. Some of its incidents (though not its theme) were used by Universal Studios in their 1933 version of H. G. Wells' *The Invisible Man*. Most interestingly, this novel, like *Gladiator*, spawned innumerable second-rate imitations in pulp magazines and movie scripts. Perhaps that is why some of it seems so familiar to contemporary readers. All things considered, *The Murderer Invisible* is one of the best of the early books and deservedly sold well in a 1959 paperback edition.

II *A Breakthrough in* Redbook

The first of Wylie's fourteen novels for *Redbook* was *The Footprint of Cinderella*, a five-part serial that was printed in book form in 1931 and re-issued in 1959 as *9 Rittenhouse Square*. Based on an idea suggested by Edwin Balmer, it is a modernized American version of the traditional story of the poor and virtuous girl who, despite the efforts of her wicked female relatives, wins the heart of the prince. In Wylie's tale, the heroine, Janet Jamison, is really the daughter of a Philadelphia aristocrat; but she had been secretly kidnapped as an infant and brought up by an unsuspecting couple in the Midwest. In place of the evil stepmother is Janet's snobbish aunt, Chloe LaForge-Leigh, who had substituted another child (Muriel Leigh) for her. The role of the fairy godmother is carried out by an attorney, Douglas Avery; his son, Barney Avery, becomes the prince and uses a footprint made at the girl's birth, instead of a glass slipper, to identify her.

Using this seemingly unpromising material, Wylie fashioned a novel that became his first popular success and one that quickly earned him the reputation of being one of the best writers of magazine fiction. Farrar and Rinehart brought out a hard-cover edition in July, and *Redbook* began publishing Wylie's stories regularly, proudly prefacing them with the statement that he was the well-known author of *The Footprint of Cinderella*. Other magazines became eager to see his work, and thus, with the help of his own "fairy godfather," Wylie found himself living in his own Cinderella story of success and recognition.

An examination of the novel shows that Wylie had, indeed, mastered the requirements of light fiction. He had found the two basic themes that he would use with endless variations in subsequent popular works—the triumph of Midwestern innocence over

Eastern sophistication and the rise to wealth of the virtuous. His characters are sharply defined but simplified versions of real-life people—in other words, they are easily recognizable types. It should be noted, however, that most of these personages seem far more real than those which one normally finds in escape fiction; the explanation lies in Wylie's exceptional skill, already displayed in his serious novels, in using individualized lines of dialogue to suggest the personality traits of the speakers.

Wylie's plot is full of suspense, endless complications, and surprising turns of events—not to mention an engaging love story and a happy ending in which the villains are soundly defeated and one of them (Muriel) is converted to a life of virtue. Wylie even manages to make the exchange of the babies seem credible; however, the final scene, in which Chloe is driven into making a confession, destroys the illusion of reality in part because it sounds too much like the standard ending of murder mysteries and also because, in real life, women like her never confess to anything.

Wylie's main purpose in writing *Cinderella* was to entertain, but he also used the novel to set forth a number of his unconventional views about sexual morality, traditional religious beliefs, and the domineering woman in modern America. Most magazine editors would have rejected such controversial material, fearing that it might result in cancelled subscriptions; but Balmer, hoping to attract the under-thirty generation to *Redbook*, deliberately advertised *Cinderella* as "completely modern" fiction by a younger writer "who graphically and gayly reports the amazing realities of our day."[2] The experiment worked: the success of *Cinderella* proved that there was room in *Redbook* for at least one social satirist and critic of contemporary attitudes and values. At last Wylie had a larger audience for his ideas than his books had reached. He was still, by more recent standards, extremely limited in what he could say, but over the next decade, in novels like *As They Reveled, Too Much of Everything, Smoke Across the Moon, Home from the Hills,* and *No Scandal!,* he was able to print stories on subjects that were taboo in all other periodicals.

Wylie rather cleverly promulgated his views in *Cinderella* by assigning them to his attractive characters and by having their antagonists illustrate the evils which he was attacking. The hero, Barney Avery, for example, "didn't believe in a future life. He believed God was merely growing and living. But he did believe in trying to do one's best." Janet Jamison, the heroine and a "nice" girl, had "attained a certain emancipation" in matters of sexual behavior by "parking" with young men from her home town, yet appears to have emerged from the experience with no damage to her morals, with a wholesome interest in sex, and with a fund of practical information that would have been denied her under the chaperone system.

Old Mr. Avery obviously illustrates Wylie's view of how parents should regard their puzzling offspring—with confidence that, underlying their eccentric behavior, there is a fundamental honesty and hatred of hypocrisy, a refusal to enter "into the petty compromise, the moral and social crookedness of life." Their children "go wrong" only when their parents are themselves poor examples of honor and integrity, have neglected their duty to guide their children's moral development, or have deliberately inculcated in them a selfish and materialistic code of behavior. Thus Muriel Leigh cannot really be blamed for her actions or her belief that she is a superior being whom men must serve: her father (like Wylie's) had devoted his life to a solitary grieving for his dead wife and had allowed the child to be corrupted by her aunt's views on love, marriage, and responsibility to others. Years later, after much philosophical speculation, Wylie would return to this same idea and assert that the moral directive that underlies all others (and is in fact nature's commandment) is that the young be properly cared for and educated for life.

The villain of *Cinderella* is a personage known to every person who has ever heard of *Generation of Vipers:* it is Mom. Wylie would not invent the term for a dozen years, and Chloe LaForge-Leigh is a spinster, but otherwise the conception is already complete.[3] Chloe is Mom, that real-life source of mother-in-law jokes, that perversion of everything that nature intended a mother to be, that smug hypocrite who hides herself in the mantle woven by the deeds of real women, that most repulsive of beings, the female without any sexual feelings and, in place of them, a cold and empty thrust of will and malice.

Wylie's portrayal of Chloe overshadows all of his other achievements in *Cinderella;* she is, in fact, one of his most unforgettable characters, and she is drawn with every device at his command. Her speeches are ingrained with her insufferable snobbery. Her physical appearance is a mirror of her personality: her obesity suggests a fundamental grossness of mind rather than the aristocratic refinement she claims to have inherited from noble ancestors; and her face, unwashed but coated with rouge and powder, reveals her obsession with preserving outward appearances. Her actions toward the other characters, of course, best dramatize her worst qualities: her willfullness that drives her to achieve her own ends at any cost to others, spitefulness and utter disregard for moral considerations, the resourcefulness, cunning, and indefatigable patience that make her such a dangerous opponent, and, most infuriating, an unbearable hypocrisy and self-righteousness.

In order to discover the sources of Chloe's monstrous behavior, Wylie probes her private thoughts like a Freudian analyst and comments at length on his discoveries. Her views on the relations between the sexes are the products of her Victorian upbringing: "decent" women are vessels of purity who do not have sexual feelings; marriage is a loveless arrangement in which the female submits to male lust in return for material compensation; and any woman, whether a mother or not, is entitled to reverence, special privileges, and a soft life. Chloe does not realize that her secret craving for lurid newspaper accounts of violence and death is a sign of a sexually unfulfilled life. Nor can she ever admit to herself that she possesses a giant inferiority complex growing out of her lifelong unattractiveness to men—or that her self-aggrandizement and lust for power are an overcompensation for those feelings.

Her hatred of her beautiful sister-in-law and her attempt to dispose of her niece are the results of a jealousy as all-consuming as her own lack of self-esteem. Looking even deeper into her psyche, Wylie finds another cause for her jealousy: an incestuous attachment to her brother. This aberration in turn explains her extreme prudishness. Having been conditioned by her Victorian upbringing to regard even normal sexual feelings as shameful, Chloe cannot ever begin to cope with her discovery about herself, forces it into her subconscious mind, and protects herself from suspicion by a public contempt for any expression of sexual love. Her ignorance of herself is nearly complete, and for that reason she, and women like her, are a nearly uncontrollable destructive force in society.

Although *Cinderella* sets forth with great effectiveness an impressive array of social commentary and psychological insights, the novel is a failure. More accurately, it miscarries because of the amount and nature of such material. Wylie had already, on several occasions, used a work of fiction as a vehicle for the presentation of his ideas; but in those instances the basic story had also been serious in tone. In this case, his choice of a plot was a critical error: *Cinderella* is a light-hearted love story with both a premise and a conclusion that we can not—and are not expected to—take seriously. Yet the book cannot be enjoyed on that level because the weighty matters on Momism and Freudian aberrations require a thoughtful approach to all the events that occur. In short, *Cinderella*, and the reader, suffer from a real "conflict of interests" on Wylie's part.

In retrospect, we can see that there were strong emotional reasons behind Wylie's attempt to turn Balmer's little tale into a denunciation of those elements in American life of which he disapproved. Certainly he was, either consciously or unconsciously, repeating the pattern already established in books like *Gladiator* and *The Murderer Invisible*. But, more important, he was seething inwardly with feelings that he needed to express, particularly those about women. It is quite likely that an encounter with an obdurate older woman like Chloe (perhaps the immovable Flora May Holly) triggered the wrath that he had been storing up for decades against every one of her type—an anger that began with Grandmother Wylie and the meddling middle-aged females in his father's churches. A more easily identifiable source of his irritation is Sally Wylie, who was at least one of the models for the self-centered Muriel Leigh. In any case, Wylie's marital problems were creating in him a high level of frustration that often was transferred to other objects as well. *Cinderella* gave him temporary relief; but, since his relationship with Sally would only worsen over the next few years, the eruption that took place in *Finnley Wren* in 1934 was inevitable.

III   *Three Murder Mysteries*

The first book to which Balmer and Wylie both signed their names was *Five Fatal Words*, which first appeared in November, 1931, and the next year in hard cover. The Chicago Tribune News Syndicate was planning a contest to increase circulation: the idea was to publish a hundred-thousand-word mystery story in installments and to offer prizes to the readers who solved the mystery first. Balmer and Wylie applied for the job of producing such a work, and, when they were asked their price, Balmer audaciously set it at twenty-five thousand dollars (about three times what they might expect to receive). To Balmer's astonishment, the bid was accepted, and they left the editorial offices, Wylie gleeful and Balmer with his knees shaking. *The Golden Hoard* (1933) and *The Shield of Silence* (1935) were also done for the same syndicate, with Balmer devising the plot, whose intriguing clues were planted in each of the fifteen episodes. They shared the profits equally, an arrangement Wylie soon found unfair.

Two of the three novels more than fulfilled the specifications of the editors who commissioned them. *Five Fatal Words* has seemingly real people who are portrayed not by direct authorial comment but by dialogue in which each has a distinctive, individualized sound. The best is *The Shield of Silence*, with its detailed picture of contemporary Chicago and characters who come alive because of the use of psychology to explain their actions. Wylie is especially successful in using long sustained conversations between sets of characters for exposition and to advance the narrative. All of these qualities explain why the young author soon became one of the most sought-after creators of tales of this type and why his name was always displayed prominently on the covers of magazines containing them.

IV   When Worlds Collide

Of all the Balmer-Wylie collaborations, the most popular and famous was *When Worlds Collide* (1932); today it is the only book for which Balmer is remembered, while few people are aware that Wylie had a part in it. As usual, the idea was Balmer's: the destruction of the earth by one of a pair of planets that wander into the solar system, and the attempts of a scientist to build a spaceship that will carry a selected few to possible safety on the second of the intruders. When Wylie began the project, he immediately—and characteristically—consulted some of his astronomer friends, who computed for him the size of the planets and their trajectories. As late as 1966, Wylie spoke with pride of the accuracy of the astrophysics in *When Worlds Collide*, though he admitted to one serious error—he had made the sky of Bronson Beta green, not blue.

When Worlds Collide was one of the most successful science-fiction stories ever written. When it began appearing as a serial in *Bluebook* in September, 1932, it doubled that magazine's circulation. It was a heavy seller in book form in 1933 and has stayed in print in various forms in which a total of 504,046 copies were sold. In 1951 (at long last), it was made into a movie—incidentally, one of the few movie versions of Wylie's work of which he approved. It is still a staple of lending libraries and is considered by scholars a classic in the field of science-fiction.

The Wylie fan who expects to find well-drawn characters or stylistic excellence in this novel will be disappointed, but other aspects are more typical of his work. The plot is genuinely suspenseful, and the detailed treatment of tidal waves, massacres, hand-to-hand battles between mobs and National Guardsmen (an interesting foreshadowing of scenes in *Tomorrow!* and *Triumph*), earthquakes, volcanic eruptions, and the death of the earth itself is a genuine feat of the imagination. Equally familiar is Wylie's misanthropy, which rivals the harshest pages of *Vipers*. The masses of men, he says, are lost in selfishness and superstition, are only a short remove from savagery, and, in fact, revert to it in any situation that removes the restraint of authority or government. The only men worth saving are ones like Hendron, the physicist-psychologist-humanist who, like Wylie in *Vipers* and in *An Essay on Morals*, insists that all aspects of human life, including morality and religious beliefs, be examined with the same honesty that has made possible all of man's advances in the physical sciences.

V   After Worlds Collide

The novel was such a success—and stopped at such a dramatic point—that the reviewers and public alike demanded an immediate sequel. After some delay caused by Wylie's demand for a greater share of the profits, *After Worlds Collide* was written. Initially, Wylie planned a story in which the colonists would find and revive the former inhabitants of the planet, who had been in suspended animation for eons as their frozen planet moved through space. Balmer took over the project, rejected that idea, and introduced a whole different set of adventures. He had little knowledge of scientific matters and, not sharing Wylie's dedication to plausibility, insisted on including wholly impossible material. Still, some of the science is surely Wylie's—not just the celestial mechanics but also the strange futuristic machines found in the abandoned dome-enclosed cities. Most of the other good features of the book are probably attributable to Balmer.

VI   The Savage Gentleman

The Savage Gentleman, a fifty-thousand-word novelette, was written, probably in 1931, as a serial; but, after no one would buy it, Farrar and Rinehart issued it in hard cover in November, 1932. Wylie's original idea was to explore a kind of "infinite situation": "Suppose you didn't have all your cultural contact with the other sex and had never seen a woman. What would you do when you saw one?" Later, he decided to include the subject of "newspaper policy" in order to criticize the press for unethical use of its powers and indifference to its responsibility to the public. As the book took shape in his mind, he chose as protagonist a type he had grown fond of using—a young man of exceptional intelligence, astounding physical strength, absolute moral uprightness, and great innocence, whose special trial is an encounter with the corrupted values of modern America.

The novel begins in 1895, when Stephen Stone, a millionaire New York newspaper publisher, deliberately maroons himself on an uncharted island in the Indian Ocean. His companions are his infant son, Henry; the captain of his yacht, a talented engineer named McCobb; and his Negro servant, Jack. Stone's purpose is to educate his son in an environment free of the influence of women; embittered by the behavior of his unfaithful wife, he hopes by careful indoctrination to protect his son from similar hurt. Rescue comes in 1928, when Stone is dead. Young Henry, aged thirty-three, is returned to modern-day New York City to face his inheritance—280 million dollars, a greatly expanded chain of twenty-two newspapers and eleven banks, a clever manipulator named Vorhees, who is using the papers for political and personal gain—and the modern woman.

Henry is sickened by what appears to him to be universal corruption, a nation not worth salvaging. His problems are not helped at all by the beautiful and sexually liberated Marian Whitney, who easily seduces him and then shatters his psyche by laughing at his quaint, old-fashioned proposal of marriage to compensate her for what he had thought to be her loss of virginity. He is ready to return to the emotional security of his island when Vorhees orders him murdered. Jack thwarts the attempt, at the cost of his own life; and Henry, forgetting that he is a gentleman, runs amok like Hugo Danner and hospitalizes at least a dozen assorted thugs, crooks, and politicians. The story ends with his decision to use his papers to clean up the world and to accept Marian on her own terms, whereby she is not his property and is free to have anyone she wants as her lover.

The Savage Gentleman should never have been published, because Wylie, after firmly establishing the premises for Henry's New York adventure and after arousing the reader's expectations, is able to come up with absolutely nothing original, enlightening, or even entertaining for his hero to do. Henry gains little direct, dramatic experience with the evils of the contemporary world; instead, they are reported to him in a monologue that is really an inserted essay. Vorhees and his cohorts are never real, having been patterned on the villains in movie melodramas; and their defeat in a free-for-all fight is too simplistic a solution to the social problem they represent (not to mention impossible, since Henry is not Hugo Danner).

Most disappointingly, after preparing the hero for the confrontation with the opposite sex, Wylie barely begins to explore the many possibilities inherent in the situation. He reduces the whole subject to a slanted and very unconvincing argument for the right of a woman to sexual freedom, an effort which fails, primarily because Wylie does not recognize that his "heroine" is, like Sally Wylie, a hypocrite who uses the legitimate demands of women to justify all her cruel, willful, and self-indulgent behavior.

The Savage Gentleman is not without some virtues. The colonizing and exploring of the island, especially the discovery of the ruins of an ancient civilization, are nearly as entertaining as the similar accounts in the books which were Wylie's admitted models—Defoe's *Robinson Crusoe* and Jules Verne's *The Mysterious Island*. Some readers might enjoy following the progress of the elder Stone's carefully detailed system of education, which is enlivened with anecdotes and short scenes. Also, even though the characters are the stereotypes of pulp fiction and rarely take life even in the dialogue, there are a few moments when the characters sound like people. The most delightful of them is the constantly indignant old man, Elihu Whitney, who is clearly the literary ancestor of Ricardo Jones of *Finnley Wren*.

CHAPTER 4

The Magnificent Finnley Wren

IN April, 1934, appeared *Finnley Wren*, Wylie's most original and possibly greatest novel. In one sense, it is the natural successor of *Heavy Laden* and *Babes and Sucklings*, both of which had earned him a reputation as a chronicler of the lives of the young people of his generation, the first one to experience the full impact of what it meant to be liberated from the Victorian ideas about God, marriage, and social behavior in general. Both books, though causing a small furor when they appeared, seem as mild as Sinclair Lewis' *Main Street* does today—and in fact have been quietly forgotten.

But *Finnley Wren* lives on, a furious, magnificent act of creation that is no mere document of rebellious sons or young free lovers in the 1920s and early 1930s, not just a clever satire of the absurdities of the day: it is a man's outraged outcry against those things that outlast all topicality: man's ineradicable stupidity, cruelty, and selfishness; his inescapable burden of suffering, pain, loneliness, and death; and, most of all, the lack of any meaning or explanation of his tragic fate. But, though this novel is a savage and unforgiving indictment that spares nothing and no one, it is also paradoxically an affirmation of all that is infinitely precious: courage, love, honesty, self-knowledge, beauty (whether in nature or in a human heart), and the love of life that will not permit the truly alive to "go gentle into that good night." And, not incidentally, *Finnley Wren* is a dazzling and audacious display of stylistic virtuosity and of technical ingenuity, a work which both parodies the "modern" novel and employs its methods to achieve its own ends.

Clearly, there can be no easy or simple explanation of how the book came into being, but one major factor was its author's temperament: Wylie was a volatile, easily angered, unstable, and unforgiving young egotist—as well as a sensitive, well-meaning, and intelligent one. He had had, of course, a number of experiences that had given him grounds for outbursts of rage. He had not been able to win acceptance by the literary establishment. He had not been able to solve his marital problems, and he was increasingly galled by Sally's treatment of him. But the most embittering event in his life—and probably the key one in the creation of *Finnley Wren*—had happened eight years earlier in Montclair: resentment had been building in him ever since he had unjustly been found guilty of fathering Henrietta Hammond's child. To put it simply, Wylie wanted revenge—on all of those, including his father, who had offended against him. He apparently had only been seeking the proper literary vehicle for his wrath.

All of Wylie's problems and frustrations came close to overwhelming him in the latter part of 1932, when he was living in Hollywood and was working as a script-writer for Paramount. Sally had accompanied him to the West Coast; but, when she had then returned to New York and her affairs, she left behind Karen, who was not yet a year old, for him to care for. Having few acquaintances in Hollywood, especially female ones, and tied to his house at night by his child, Wylie soon sank into a mood of melancholy, loneliness, and despair, and, underneath it all, smoldering anger. At this point, he resolved to start a new novel: "I decided to write a book about what the past years had seemed like, could have been, should have, and were not." It was, as he said in a taped interview with Keefer (August, 1966), something composed "for myself" and not, at that point, intended for publication. It was, in other words, an attempt to externalize his emotional difficulties by setting them down on paper.

The basic outline of the novel came to him at once. The main character, Finnley Wren, would be based "partly on a guy I'd known and liked named Finley [the son of the author, Finley Peter Dunne], a big guy with those looks and somewhat the same suaveness—but not really like Finnley inside." Instead, he would be much like the author, and to him Wylie gave many of his own experiences. Wylie included himself as a separate character, apparently acting on a whim, but perhaps also understanding instinctively that this device would enable him to write about Finnley with the objectivity and detachment that is missing in most autobiographical fiction.

Although Wylie did invent a great deal of the novel—and altered much of what he used—he did base a significant amount of it on real life. Finnley's disastrous encounter with Libby Maretti is almost exactly like the author's with the Hammond girl. Helen Holbein, the liberated young pseudo-intellectual who nearly destroys the hero, has so many qualities like those of Sally Wylie that it is impossible to believe the author's assertion that she was not his model. The fact that the novel is dedicated to her merely illustrates Wylie's gallant refusal to see Sally as she really was and his tendency to blame himself for their problems. Apparently, only by telling himself that Helen was a wholly invented character was he able to describe Sally truthfully.

Some of Wylie's other borrowings are less literal. Finnley's father, for example, bears no resemblance in physical appearance, athletic prowess, or profession to the Reverend Edmund Wylie, who had been pictured unmistakably in *Heavy Laden*. The cruel beating which Dr. Wren gives his son for an innocent piece of blasphemy is, however, based on a similar event in Wylie's life, and the general hatred of both hero and author for their male parents is identical. All of the portraits of Helen Holbein's intellectual friends are imaginary, Wylie recalled, except for the young man who committed incest with his sister: he was in real life an acquaintance at Princeton.

The two main examples of completely invented material are Finnley's delightful romance with Hope and the visit to the Dwyer home, where the weekend guests are permitted to practice free love in the interest of science. The first episode is obviously Wylie's idea of what a marriage ought to be—and perhaps reflects the illusions he entertained when he married Sally. The second is a typical Wylie joke, a far-fetched sexual fantasy. He did not intend it to be taken seriously, and, years later, would be astounded when wife-swapping orgies became one of the aspects of the sexual revolution of the 1960s.

The baroque title (in eight different kinds and sizes of type, both red and black) is a fairly complete account of the story he produced: *Finnley Wren: His Notions and Opinions together with a Haphazard History of His Career and Amours in these Moody Years, as well as Sundry Rhymes, Fables, Diatribes and Literary Misdemeanors. A novel in a new manner.* Set in New York City and a country house in Connecticut, it is a first-person account by a fictional novelist named Philip Wylie of his forty-eight hour acquaintance with the title character. During this period, Wylie spends most of his time listening to Finnley telling the story of his life and enlarging on his opinions—or to other characters who give him their views of the remarkable Finnley.

The story begins on Friday afternoon with Wylie and Wren's first and accidental meeting in a New York speakeasy. Over a succession of highballs Finnley tells of his father, Dr. Gordon Wren; his betrayal in adolescence by Jessica, his steady girl; a second betrayal, this time by a working-class girl, Libby Maretti, who falsely accused him of being the father of her unborn child; and the reaction of his father and the entire hypocritical community, which forced him to leave home. Later, over dinner in a restaurant, Wylie listens to the story of his meeting and courtship of Hope Jones, the daughter of an eccentric advertising man. Then he is invited to go with Finnley to spend the weekend at the home of Donald Dwyer near New Haven; he accepts, goes with him to his penthouse, and, while waiting for Finnley to change his clothes, reads two of his "epistles" (obscurely symbolic fantasies), and sees a portrait of Helen Holbein, Wren's second wife.

After arriving at the Dwyers', Wylie is appropriated by a beautiful woman named Estelle, who tries to seduce him in her bedroom by removing her clothes. Wylie, preferring to be faithful to his absent wife, elicits from her instead information about Helen Holbein and is told how she decided to dramatize her feminist views—and become the cynosure of her circle of New York pseudo-intellectuals—by having a child out of wedlock, the father being selected for eugenic reasons. Although Wylie resists Estelle's blandishments, later in the evening, while in an alcoholic haze, he is overcome by the charms of Flora who is seemingly a moronic chorus girl but is actually, as he discovers the next day, a very intelligent obstetrician.

On Saturday morning Finnley tells Wylie of his most horrifying experience: a forest fire in Canada which killed and terribly injured scores of people. He also reveals how his beloved Hope died as another victim of fire in a pointless accident. His views on death and the inevitability of horror and human suffering merge into his bitter denunciation of three-quarters of contemporary Americans as lost in folly and ignorance.

In the remaining pages of the novel, Finnley explains that, before he met Wylie, he had been nearly deranged by Helen's betrayal; but now, having cured himself by finding a patient listener (Wylie), he has discovered the origins of his anxieties and frustrations; and, after undoing some of Helen's evil, he now can live a normal life. He has come to realize, he claims, that he is not at all an unusual person. Wylie is disappointed, because maturity has banished the magic of Finnley Wren. The change, however, is not permanent: months later he receives a phone call from Wren, whose opening words about a recent adventure (involving a countess and a dish of hash) end the novel in mid-sentence.

The various techniques and literary devices used by Wylie in the novel range from the functional to the merely ornamental. Point of view is the most important; basically, he uses three. The framework story is a first-person narrative, with "Wylie" as narrator. Finnley's monologues are reported by Wylie; but, since Wren sometimes talks for pages without interruption by "Wylie," the effect is of a second first-person narrative within the first-person account. The novel also has sections of third-person narrative told from the point of view of the omniscient author.

Another of Wylie's techniques is his insertion and extended quotation of various pieces of written material, most of them from Finnley's hand. These compositions reveal the hero's character as well as provide a change of pace for the reader—and all of them are delightful in themselves. In fact, Wylie may have included them more for their own sake than to characterize Wren. He would again use this kind of insertion in a number of later novels, including *Night Unto Night, The Disappearance,* and *Opus 21.*

The style of *Finnley Wren* is an awesome *tour de force*, the most extravagant display of vocabulary Wylie was ever to make. Illustrations of Finnley's varied diction are almost too easy to find. The nonstandard English includes "the brashest slang" and many of the well-known profane and obscene terms; "son of a bitch" was the most shocking one to the audience of 1934. Wren also draws upon scientific and technological terms. His formal vocabulary, a reflection of his extensive reading and awareness of beauty in language, is made up of many of the unusual "big" words with which Wylie had been ornamenting his novels for years. Here, however, they are appropriate because they are entirely consistent with the extravagant nature of the speaker. Wren is also fond of intermingling words from his different vocabularies to produce astonishing and bizarre juxtapositions.

The main aim of the novel was to give the reader a complete exposure to the personality of the title figure. To do that, Wylie drew upon the methods he had perfected in earlier books: Finnley himself tells us what he is; other characters comment on him; some of the characters in the flashbacks state their views; there are reports of the world's view of him; and "Wylie," too, draws his conclusions. We also have the opportunity of seeing Finnley's actions in various key events in his life, and he reports, apparently quite honestly, on his thoughts at these times. But vastly more important is the constant barrage on our ears of his opinions. The overall effect is the creation of an extraordinarily believable character—perhaps Wylie's best. There is no one like him in fiction, and perhaps no one in real life, except Wylie himself, who supplied Finnley with many of his own qualities and opinions. Yet every reader who has ever responded to this novel has recognized in Wren much of himself. Thus, this unique being is also, paradoxically, a perennially universal one.

We would hardly expect a "one-man show" like this novel to have well-developed or even memorable supporting characters. Nevertheless, there are four remarkable ones in *Finnley Wren:* Dr. Gordon Wren, Helen Holbein, Hope Jones, and Ricardo Jones—Hope's father. Hope and Ricardo are drawn with love and affection, but the other portraits, inspired by Wylie's raw hatred of their prototypes, are among the most despicable beings in literature. Doctor Wren is characterized by every method except his thoughts, but the savage use of his physical appearance to discredit him borders on genius. His hypocrisy is summed up by his clothes: he wears a well-cut suit over frayed underwear, a girdle, and a "moldered jockstrap." The true nature of his spiritual condition is suggested by a Swiftian catalogue of his boddily defects; and, when we are given a list of the eleven classes of germs that live on various parts of his anatomy, our feelings of revulsion toward him are insurmountable.

Helen Holbein—the cunning, lying, self-centered pseudo-intellectual and self-made parody of the "modern" woman—is a much more complex being, one quite capable of deceiving Finnley about her true nature. Men usually are incapable of correct judgments of women like her—until it is too late—but other women are much more acute, and Wylie quite shrewdly allows Estelle to expose Helen. Otherwise, he lets her actions speak for themselves, and their evidence needs no comment.

Finnley Wren owes much of its notoriety to the fact that in it Wylie was able, for the first time, to speak his mind without restraint on everything that irritated him. At one point, Finnley

says, "Everything's wrong—wrong—wrong. Hideously wrong. It
has always been wrong. It will take thousands and thousands of
years to make it right. It will take forever. And yet—it could be set
right—if it weren't for the plethora of greedy fools. Nitwits. Nin-
compoops. How I hate people!" The indictment seems too sweeping to fit into one book, but only when we try to list the objects of
satire in *Finnley Wren* do we realize fully how many targets Wylie
has hit. Not only Finnley but also Estelle, a nameless sad man who
appears in tears five times, and "Wylie" himself contribute to the
diatribes. On one occasion, Wren reads aloud an eight-page article
someone sent him—and that piece is an attack also. Of course, some
subjects receive greater attention than others—these are exposed in
their shortcomings by being dramatized in episodes—while others
are dismissed with a mere epithet.

The following is a mere sampling of the pungent opinions that
grace the novel. The principle of giving everyone a vote—both the
foolish and the wise—has caused the failure of representative
government. The actions of Christians expose their complete lack of
any religion whatsoever, especially when tenets of their faith are
criticized. So-called sex offenders are punished extravagantly for actions that are so widespread as to be correctly called normal.
Newspapers are printed to make money by appealing to the lusts of
a lascivious, thrill-seeking people. American businessmen dedicate
their lives to inventing gadgets and then creating an artificial desire
or "need" for them.

The educational system is dedicated to presenting facts without
correlation or explanation, to instilling a thousand lies instead of the
hard truths, to avoiding the discoveries and implications of science,
and to making sex and the body a subject of shame. The chief result
of the feminist movement has been to convince women that they
must abandon their function as mothers and turn themselves into
men in order to find freedom and happiness; men have encouraged
women's latent selfishness by giving them every material comfort
they want. The *New Yorker* set—like any similar group of intellectuals—has no real claim to superiority: they are "run-of-the-mill
human beings." Finnley's most compelling polemic is addressed to
the stupidity of the great American masses: "The melting pot has
turned out to be a cesspool." He therefore proposes the passage of
the "Ass-reduction Act," under which seventy-five percent of the
population would be legally executed as not fit to live, not to mention reproduce.

If Wylie's views of his fellow Americans, especially of their self-righteousness, were even partially valid, then *Finnley Wren* was certain to offend a greater proportion of the population than had any other book written on this continent. In fact, during the Cold War of the 1950s, the novel, along with *Generation of Vipers,* was excluded from United States Information Agency libraries in foreign countries as too anti-American.

But whether or not we feel that Wylie is right, it is still possible to enjoy the diatribes. In the first place, the attacks are so cleverly phrased, so uninhibited in expression and vehemence, so imaginative, so Shakespearean in their uses of the resources of the language, that they compel admiration. At times, we become aware, too, that Wylie is consciously enjoying his deployment of the language, and this knowledge somehow is cathartic: his ridicule and vituperation are the actions of a strong and confident man, not a victim; and we therefore find ourselves believing, against our wills, that his words are capable of changing the world.

It should be noted, too, that Wylie's use of Wren as a *persona* tends to disarm criticism. Since most of the attacks are delivered by Wren and his friends, the reader gets the impression that Wylie does not necessarily agree with what is said. In fact, he, in some of his comments, seems to approve of Wren's change at the end of the story into a calm and uncritical ordinary person. Even the characters themselves at times satirize their own views as having become the clichés of intellectuals and pseudo-intellectuals. Wren, for instance, after reading aloud an article criticizing businessmen, throws it away, commenting, "Nonsense! Sheer nonsense . . . . Give any writer in North America what is called an 'angle' and he will produce just such ringing half-truths." Nevertheless, the case has been stated for the "prosecution"; as in a trial, although a judge instructs the jury to disregard certain statements which they have just heard, they will not be able to forget them.

The reader cannot efface from his mind another impression made by this book, namely that the life of every human being is in constant peril of unthinkable horrors. Wylie put into *Finnley Wren* his most unbearable scenes. They are understated and—to use Wylie's description of Finnley's own style—couched in "words so passionately compressed that they emerge small, hard and individually alive." After a forest fire sweeps a Canadian town, Finnley attempts to aid the horribly burned survivors. One woman has a face "that looked like an ill-butchered ham cooked too long, and in that red and gummy gobbet she opened a hole from which she emitted a long, agonized shriek." Another still-living being found another, more horrendous fate: "the wolves had been eating him."

The torments of the mind are not omitted. After Finnley quietly tells how his wife died in his arms, he "suddenly yelled at the top of his mighty voice and threw himself at my feet and began to kick and bite the earth and to beat it with his fists." No reader of this novel will feel safe ever afterward, for Wylie has made him share his own private nightmare: death and horror are the unavoidable and primary fact of life. As Finnley sums it up, "My God, it's a wonder people can live at all when you think what happens to them in the light of what they are taught to believe." None of this suffering has meaning or even a pattern. Yet, because it is so universal, it provides a kind of makeshift justice: the guilty who escape punishment do so only for a time; ultimately, they will suffer enough in the ordinary course of human experience to satisfy all the longings for vengeance in the hearts of their victims. Thus, in the closing pages of the novel, Wylie with grim pleasure shows the fate of those who sinned against Finnley. Dr. Wren is aging alone; Libby is a sodden alcoholic; Helen finds her hold loosening on her current victim; his first girl friend, her beauty gone, nurses her fourth child and flounders in hideous domesticity.

Astonishingly—and perhaps necessarily in a story so full of anguish—*Finnley Wren* is one of Wylie's funniest books. Most of the humor comes from his satiric comments on whatever he dislikes. The style itself produces comedy through its self-conscious exaggerations. And, as always in Wylie, there is also plenty of slapstick, as when Finnley pursues an intruding photographer down the street and repeatedly "kicked him so hard that he was lifted clear off the ground," and when an amiable drunk "fell face forward, narrowly missing one of the Whittington cats." Such moments make both life and *Finnley Wren* bearable.

In the 1960s, when Wylie had decided to concentrate on nonfictional "idea-books," an editor turned down a new work and suggested that he write another like *Finnley Wren*. Wylie refused, because he did not want to repeat himself, to do something he had done before. The editor was correct in his belief that the novel is one of the three books where Wylie reached greatness; but he did not understand that, in the words of Truman Capote's friend in "A Christmas Memory," "There's never two of anything." Wylie had learned that truth when, years earlier, he had tried to "finish it" but had to give up; he saw that everything he had to say had been said—and could not be said again or better.

CHAPTER 5

The Late 1930s

I N the nearly eight years between *Finnley Wren* and *Vipers,* Wylie wrote at a prodigious rate, but produced nothing of their stature. Deeply disappointed that he had not received the literary acclaim which he deserved for *Finnley,* he petulantly declared that henceforth he would confine his efforts to making money with "potboilers." To a considerable degree, he carried out that resolve; his annual income often approached the $40,548 earned in 1935. Movie scripts written in Hollywood, serialized novels in the best-paying magazines, a succession of murder mysteries (most notably, seven novel-length tales for *American,* which gave a record-breaking $2,500 for the *Paradise Canyon Mystery),*[1] and finally the Crunch and Des series in *Saturday Evening Post* occupied his attention and would have made him a rich man if he had not spent the money as fast as it came in.

During this period, despite Wylie's public disclaimers, he also pursued his other career, that of social critic and satirist, usually in the one periodical that encouraged such work, *Redbook* (though it was also one of his best customers for normal magazine fare). *As They Reveled, Too Much of Everything, Home from the Hills, Smoke Across the Moon,* and *No Scandal!* were all attempts to promulgate, though in a somewhat subdued manner, many of the same opinions and ideas that are found in *Finnley Wren.* Moreover, judging by his letters to Harold Ober and the quality of the writing in those works, Wylie was still hoping to show the critics that he was to be taken seriously as a literary man.

The events in his personal life at this time were hardly conducive to writing. After the failure of *Finnley,* he often fell into moods of deep depression during which his drinking was that of a confirmed alcoholic and his behavior was extremely violent. His marriage to Sally ended in 1937 in a Reno divorce following a financial settlement that gave her most of the property and the custody of Karen. The greatest disaster, however, occurred in 1936, when his trip to Russia culminated in the mysterious death of his young half-brother, Ted, who was probably murdered by Communist agents. Philip was left partially paralyzed from a debilitating illness he had contracted in Russia; and, worse, he was riddled with guilt feelings over Ted's fate.

Still, these years also saw a turning point in Wylie's life. He overcame the paralysis with physical therapy, and he began consulting a capable Jungian psychiatrist, who helped him sort out his problems. Even the divorce was a positive act, since it opened the way for a new and fulfilling relationship with Ricky Ballard, whom he married in 1938 and who became the emotional rock on which he built the rest of his life.[2] Another crucial event occurred in this period: in October, 1937, Wylie met Carl Jung and became deeply immersed in the philosophical ideas that would inspire some of his most important books. As a result of these happenings, the later 1930s did not become the wasted years they might have been.

I The Smiling Corpse

One excellent example of Wylie as a humorist is *The Smiling Corpse*, a thirty-five-thousand-word novelette published anonymously in March, 1935. Based on an idea proposed by one of his friends, Bernard A. Bergman, this lively and ingenious murder mystery also serves as a vehicle for satire on the genre itself; on the personalities, methods, and styles of four famous mystery writers and their fictional detectives; and on the personalities and achievements of outstanding figures in the contemporary New York literary and publishing scene.

The Smiling Corpse opens with a preface by the narrator, John Ballantine, a Hollywood star and a long-time murder mystery fan, who summarizes the methods used in the works of the four leading authors of the day. Then follows a "Who's Who" that contains the names of ninety-one of the people about to appear in the novel, with a brief, often caustic description of each. The story itself begins with the discovery that the guest of honor at a publisher's literary tea has been murdered and is lying dead in the shower with a grin on his frozen countenance. Despite their protests, the hundred guests, all the biggest names in the literary set, are locked in by a sergeant on the homicide squad, who begins an immediate investigation. Among the guests are G. K. Chesterton, S. S. Van Dine, Dashiell Hammet, and Sax Rohmer. Each one begins his own search for the murderer by using the techniques of his world-famous fictional detective.

The novelette is tremendously entertaining in every way, and especially in its plot. Actually, at least six subplots occur simultaneously; each has its own characters and developing complications, and all of them are engrossing. Yet, despite the multiplicity of events, the reader never becomes confused and, in truth, is hardly even aware of the plot's complexity because the author uses brief, strategically placed summaries as reminders of what has happened in earlier chapters.

The main source of humor is the delightful, light-hearted, and knowledgeable parodies of the exploits of "Father Brown," "Philo Vance," "Sam Spade," and "Fu Manchu"; equally funny, but often barbed with malice, are the lampoons of such notables as Harold Ross, Clare Boothe Brokaw, and Alexander Woollcott and of the Left-wing literary critics, Clifton Fadiman, Burton Rascoe, John Chamberlain, and Herschel Brickell. These passages sound like the Wylie of *Generation of Vipers*—and with good reason: this was the crowd who had given *Finnley Wren* no recognition at all. This oversight on their part had confirmed Wylie's suspicions of them: they were not equipped by education or taste to pass judgment on a work's literary merits; they perused only those books relevant to the "class-struggle" and the Marxist line, and they turned their backs on those outside their clique. Now, in *The Smiling Corpse*, Wylie was getting his revenge. Yet, as has often been true, what Wylie said in anger was nevertheless very close to the truth.

II *The Sexual Revolution: A Revisionist View*

In December, 1935, *Redbook* published a fifty-thousand-word novel, *One Love at a Time*. It was Wylie's first long work for the magazine since *The Footprint of Cinderella* in 1931, and his name was emblazoned for the first time on the front cover of the magazine—indicating both the growing importance of Wylie's name and the editor's opinion of his latest work. *One Love at a Time* was an "abbreviated" (in reality expurgated) version of a seventy-thousand-word novel, *As They Reveled*, which was released as a book in March of the following year.

On January 19, 1936, writing to Harold Ober, Wylie spoke of the book "as a treatise on morals with a very bitter lesson." Those who had read *Finnley Wren,* with its advocacy of a sexual revolution, were undoubtedly astounded by the theme of this new novel. In it, Wylie asserts that the New Morality, which had relegated fidelity in marriage to the unenlightened past, has failed in practice because even the most "enlightened" moderns feel sexual jealousy as strongly as their ancestors did. This dangerous emotional response is so deeply rooted in the culture that the New Morality is bringing disaster to many of its adherents.

Wylie had arrived at this conclusion through observation of his own acquaintances and especially from his own experience. As we have noted, his marriage to Sally was turning him into an alcoholic; and, after the apparent failure of *Finnley Wren,* he began consulting Dr. Archibald Strong, an analyst, in an attempt to gain perspective. Why, he wanted to know, did his wife's affairs, some of which he encouraged and even financed, make him unhappy? Why did she resent his indiscretions while insisting upon her own freedom? The analyst helped him gain insight into himself and into the nature of the problem, and one direct result was *As They Reveled,* in which he explores the effect of the New Morality on a representative group of people and, for the most part, lets the book prove that he had been promulgating for years a thesis whose ramifications he had not understood. Such a confession of error—or partial error—requires great honesty on the part of the confessor; but such unflinching integrity was always a basic element in Wylie's character.

The book is a "novel of manners" in which the events are mostly the result of the interactions of nine people. The chief characters are Alice and Wally Traves, who, after eight years of a conventional marriage, move into a house in Wycherley, Connecticut. The three neighboring couples are all vocal adherents of the modern sexual morality, which considers adultery natural and even healthful, if viewed in a mature way.

Alice, who is shocked and yet determined to be modern, tries to act "grown-up" when Wally is drawn to Sari Larch, a ravishing and often ravished redhead, whose behavior her husband, Fred Larch, a Wall Street broker, views complacently since she does not object to his women friends. Wally is understandably enthusiastic about the sexual freedom which the new code offers him after eight years of dull domesticity. Alice, despite her jealousy, tries to be a good sport.

She acts on the advice of Stuyvesant Jones, the resident intellectual and wit, and his wife, Sheila, who is a militant member of various reform groups and, in particular, the ones that advocate freedom for women. Stuy has had occasional affairs, with the full knowledge of Sheila, who, for some reason, has never taken a lover of her own. The fourth couple, Charley and Annabelle Everest, are an odd pair. He is a traveling salesman with only a high school education and a taste for cheap girls. Annabelle, a minor Philadelphia debutante, has an inhibited life as the mother of the only two children in the little colony; but, under Sheila's tutelage, she has added the rules of the New Morality to her code.

Nothing much happens in the story, except talk, until a catalyst arrives—Sari's cousin from Georgia, Claudette Hinkle. She is the essence of the Southern teaser—a hard drinking, vicious, malicious slut who uses her hot-looking body, affected drawl, and bleached hair to attract and control any male in sight who might be capable of satisfying her whims. At first, she is disconcerted by the code of the little group—since she enjoys most of all the wrecking of marriages and the humiliating of wives. But intuitively she realizes that these people are not really different and that her talents as a troublemaker will have plenty of opportunity to function.

She is right, for, by the end of the summer, the little colony of sexual liberals has been torn apart by all the untidy emotions that accompany adultery everywhere else. One nasty divorce, two separations, many bruised egos, and some physical injuries prove that the New Morality is a false god. Though some of the people in the novel manage to carry off infidelity without harm to themselves or others, there are obviously many more who should have left it alone. Wylie's theme is enunciated by Stuy Jones late in the novel: "Maybe it took more character than most people had, to live as Sheila insisted people should. Or more civilization. Certainly more restraint. Perhaps—in a thousand years—people from a different environment, a different childhood, with a new set of reasons for living."

The actors in this moral drama are presented chiefly through the extensive use of direct author statement, a method seldom relied on by twentieth century writers or, indeed, by Wylie himself in his more mature works. As a consequence, the characterization lacks the depth and reality we find in his other serious novels. In *As They Reveled*, however, this method offered the only practical solution to several problems generated by his choice of theme. In the first place, the characters were supposed to be representative or typical modern Americans, and this requirement meant that Wylie had to give each one traits that were common to a number of people. To do so, he greets each person on his first appearance in the story with what is virtually a short essay describing those qualities—attitudes, tastes, interests, background—which make him, as the case may be, a typical conventional suburbanite, a proponent of the New Morality, a misguided disciple, or one of the naturally promiscuous. Thereafter, whatever he or she does in the story is a mere illustration or amplification of that initial description.

Wylie's other main problem was to show the effect of the New Morality on these people—and that required him to explore its impact on their thoughts and attitudes as well as on their actions. Obviously, the use of dialogue or even excerpts from the characters' thoughts is a rather inefficient method if the writer has nine persons to deal with; and, even more important, it creates additional problems if these people—or even a few of them—are in the process of altering their views and are uncertain of what they actually believe. Thus, Wylie had no choice except to use authorial statements throughout the story to explain and comment carefully on their actions, words, and unspoken thoughts.

The plot of *As They Reveled* is actually a loosely linked series of episodes, and the major flaw of the novel is that the segments range in quality from excellent to unbelievably bad. The book might have been saved as a work of art if an editor had insisted that Wylie delete the parts that had failed and rewrite the novel enough to preserve the good. No one did. In fact, the only rewriting was for the *Redbook* version, which should be avoided because it omits much of the satire, slashes a page from Claudette's incomparable opening monologue, restricts Alice's indiscretion to a "mystic communion," and sends Claudette off to star in the movies.

III   Too Much of Everything

Wylie's next novel, *Too Much of Everything*, appeared as a *Redbook* serial from March through September, 1936, and in hard cover in August of the same year. The unusually long time spent on the book (five months of intense work) testifies to the importance he attached to the subject—an exploration of the causes which lay behind the most serious social problem of the time: the moral deterioration of the young.

The Bentlan family, which has "too much of everything" that money can buy, is severely shaken by the Crash of 1929, which practically wipes out the family's fortune. Eventually, after a series of near disasters in the lives of the Bentlans, some order is finally restored. The father, who decides that his future does not lie in working as a clerk in someone else's business, invents the idea of a magazine called *Money* (much like *Fortune*, apparently) in which he can use his knowledge of the business world for the benefit of the layman. The shock of losing his money and of discovering that his family is spiritually bankrupt leads him to take a firmer hand in the lives of his children. He is successful in freeing them from the influence of Della, their mother, and her totalitarian, idiotic, and old-fashioned theories of upbringing so that they may develop into sensible and unwarped individuals. The book concludes with the characters' having attained most of what they really need and with most of their problems resolved.

Wylie's attitude toward the behavior of the younger generation in *Too Much of Everything* differs sharply from that in earlier novels like *Babes and Sucklings*. Although he sympathizes with Daphne, the eldest daughter, he shows that her drinking and sexual laxness have had nothing glamorous about them; her indulgences have, in reality, brought her only humiliation at the hands of her peers and feelings of contempt from herself. He treats her brother, Jim, whose uncontrolled temper and outrage against nearly everything reminds us of Wylie himself, with sarcasm and even contempt. As for the rest of the younger generation who appear in the novel, he views them as lazy wastrels and as sensation seekers who have taken advantage of the freedoms granted them by the New Morality to corrupt themselves and each other.

In explaining what has made these people the way they are, Wylie, using Daphne as his spokesman, lays the blame squarely on the older generation. Some youngsters had been corrupted by the bad moral example of their elders and of society as a whole; others, more idealistic, had turned to drink and sex to escape from the frustration of knowing that they could neither exist in nor reform a world in which business, politics, and every other activity were dominated by blatant and cynical immorality. Most parents did not even know how much trouble their children were in because they were too busy with their pursuit of money and materialistic goods.

This novel is clearly the product of a period when Wylie was seriously evaluating his own life and trying to understand why so much of it had been such a mess. In *Too Much of Everything*, Jim climaxes a sophomoric tirade against religion by punching a minister in the eye; the minister refuses to retaliate on the grounds that he had, in a sense, provoked the immature youngster. Such an incident, in which the clergyman proves to be the better man, would never have appeared in an earlier story. Wylie was searching for answers—and rejecting errors of the past was the first step. He had not "sold out" his principles for *Redbook's* money.

Too Much of Everything, despite the author's sincerity and his meaningful theme, is not a successful novel, mostly because of its unnatural-sounding dialogue and its poorly drawn characters. Only Della, the uncontrollable and impossible wife and mother, a close relative of Chloe in *Cinderella* and the epitome of Momism, is consistently and compellingly real. The book's weaknesses were, oddly enough, not apparent to Harold Ober and Edwin Balmer, who told Wylie that it was "the best piece of magazine writing you have done." They were quite astonished when it sold only a few thousand copies and was promptly forgotten.

IV *A Superlative Romance*

In the December, 1936, issue of *Redbook* appeared *Second Honeymoon*, a fifty-thousand-word novel which the editors announced as "a gay and sophisticated romance against the glamorous background of pleasure-mad Florida" by "the brilliant author of *Too Much of Everything*." Perhaps the most effective aspect of the story (the plot is merely a variation on the conventional love triangle) is the creation of the "glamorous background." The characters go deep-sea fishing, an experience described with the same care and detail as in the later Crunch and Des stories. (This was, apparently, Wylie's first use of the deep-sea fishing motif for which he would become famous.) Other pieces of local color include the dog races, Miami at night seen from a blimp, and the bathing beaches in the stunningly bright, sea-chilled morning. The best scene is set in an expensive nightclub and suggests unerringly the pleasantly dreamy contentment and sense of well-being induced by the lush surroundings, good food, and several drinks. These exotic backgrounds helped to persuade readers that they had found a successor to Scott Fitzgerald, who had so well portrayed the romance of the idle rich of the 1920s.

Despite the plot with a happy ending, the travel poster allure of the Miami scene, and the delightful comedy in both events and dialogue, *Second Honeymoon* does contain many of Wylie's serious concerns: the typical businessman who has no genuine feelings for people, no morality except the preservation of appearances, and nothing in life but business; the attempts of women to dominate men; and the shabby power lust of "Mom."

Second Honeymoon has other good qualities. Its style is racy and fast moving, its handling of relationships between the sexes surprisingly realistic for a romance, its humor light and witty, its capturing of the languid, slow-paced undertone of sexiness in tropical Miami strangely inviting. Characterization is, quite properly, limited to the clear establishment of the types the persons belong to. In every way, it is such a pleasurable story that we regret having to admit that it is, after all, only a romance. The novel was never published in book form, but it was made into a movie a year after publication by Twentieth Century Film Corporation.

V   *The Anti-Communist:* Smoke Across the Moon

Almost alone among the writers and intellectuals of the 1930s, Wylie was not impressed in the least by either the Marxist theories of his acquaintances or the claims made by the Russians for their Communist "paradise." At a time when the United States government itself moved left of center under the New Deal; when the "proletarian novel" was the ideal of both writers and critics; when Dreiser, Dos Passos, Maxwell Anderson, Sherwood Anderson, even Hemingway, briefly, were literary Leftists, Wylie held his ground. He so completely disassociated himself from any of the Socialist or Communist organizations that in the middle 1940s, when his life was given a complete investigation by the Federal Bureau of Investigation, he received a "Q" clearance, indicating that nothing in his past cast any doubts on his loyalty to his country. Wylie was anti-Communist for many reasons. In the first place, he was a firm believer in private enterprise; second, he was repelled by the Leftists' dogmatism and demand for intellectual conformity; third, he had observed that the heartiest advocates of Russia had never been there but had accepted the doubtful evidence of Russian propaganda.[4]

In 1936, when the Russians suddenly allowed unrestricted travel inside their country, Philip and his brother, Ted, went to see "the brave new world" of Communism, a tour that included Leningrad,

Baku, and Tiflis. They found an incredibly mismanaged economy and the grim and fear-filled atmosphere of a police state. The Wylie brothers were hardly discreet about their feelings or their intention to publicize what they had seen. While they were on their way out of Russia, their railway car was inexplicably abandoned on a siding in the Odessa area for many hours; the only water was polluted, deliberately, according to Wylie; and, when they reached Warsaw, Philip had cholera. On the evening of June 27, 1936, Ted said good night to his brother, went to his room, and was next seen dead on the sidewalk six floors below his window. Wylie always believed that he had been murdered. Philip did not die of the cholera, as a doctor predicted, but it did cause a month-long paralysis in Wylie's right arm and leg. His struggles to hold on to life and then to recover his health were certainly motivated by his determination to repay the Reds for what he believed they had done.

Smoke Across the Moon, a novel serialized in the *Saturday Evening Post* starting in February, 1937, exposes five representative Americans to the same scenes which the Wylies had observed. The capitalist, the scientist, and the working girl conclude that the Communist system has failed, primarily because it offers no incentive to the individual, no material rewards for his efforts. However, the other two, a well-known labor leader and a college girl from a Left-leaning school, refuse to accept the evidence that lies before their very eyes. The girl also enabled Wylie (anticipating one of the ideas in *The Disappearance*) to denounce women's colleges. By teaching girls to regard a "career" as their goal and to scoff at the notion that a woman's real and fulfilling role is to love a man and to be a good mother to his children, they have, he says, produced a generation of troubled females who will always be dissatisfied with life.

Smoke Across the Moon was never released in book form despite the fact that it is a much better work than the *Redbook* serials that were reprinted. Its virtues are many: the descriptions of scenes in Russia are excellent reporting; the analysis of the flaws in Marxist thinking have been proved correct by history—and accepted even by the present generation of Communist economists; the style is readable and workmanlike; and there is a great deal of humor, especially in the dialogue. The novel also contains one of the ugliest episodes in any of Wylie's books: the college girl, after being rejected by the hero, renews her self-esteem by seducing a foolish young minister and then contemptuously rejects his proposal of marriage; the man hangs himself.

Admittedly, the novel has flaws. It is too obviously a vehicle for Wylie's views; the characters are not really individuals but are stereotyped as spokesmen for or representatives of various groups. Even the love story, which at first seems different and original, upon examination proves to be based on the familiar triangle plot of popular magazines. Yet, we suspect, it was its "controversial" content and not its literary lapses that caused it to be relegated forever to obscurity in a forgotten periodical.

VI   Heavy Laden *Revisited*

The "novel of the month" in *Redbook* in November, 1937, was *Home from the Hills*, a story about love, sex, morality, and religion that was certain not to be in accord with the attitudes of the conventional reader. This narrative presents the spiritual odyssey of Christian Bennon from hypocrisy and ignorance of himself to honesty and self-knowledge. In it, Wylie pillories the attitudes which he had hated in his father (the model for Bennon's career as a minister) and in the middle-class in which he had grown up. Perhaps more important, he also lays out for his readers the views which he believed were the proper attitudes. Since the novel was written when Wylie was struggling with his own emotional problems—his guilt over his brother's death, his hatred of his father, his anxiety over his shattered health, and his reaction to his divorce from Sally—the story was, in a very real sense, a working out of his personal code of ethics through the novel he was writing. Doubtless, his first experience in psychoanalysis aided him in gaining insight into what he really believed.

In view of the fact that *Home from the Hills* is a thesis novel, we might expect it to be a good sermon but a poor story; and, indeed, most of the plot defies credibility. Nevertheless, the novel "works" because the characters themselves are real, especially the two female characters, who are among Wylie's most effective portraits of women. They are fallible human beings who, nevertheless, have the qualities he most admired in the opposite sex: warm and honest sensuality, the capacity both to give and accept love, and the strength to live according to one's needs and one's convictions. The only flaw in Wylie's character portrayal is an excessive amount of direct authorial comment and "editorializing"; Wylie, it appears, could not restrain himself from attacking Bennon directly—an understandable indiscretion.

The novel is, by no means, an undiscovered masterpiece. Yet it does evoke very well the times and places in which it is set, particularly small towns in America and the war zones of Europe in 1917. The style of *Home from the Hills* is a good example of Wylie's proficiency. The narrative sections are clear (with a few exceptions), and the dialogue ranges from being merely unobtrusive to being the perfect capturing of a voice. This story is, all things considered, a very serviceable sermon.

VII No Scandal!

No Scandal!, a novel which appeared in *Redbook* in June, 1940, and surpasses any of the other works of fiction by Wylie in that periodical, is not conventional magazine material. The main plot, in which Jim Windon struggles to assert himself as a man, husband, and father and to free his two nearly grown children from the psychological influence of their mother, is, in its bare outlines, a version of *Too Much of Everything*. It is also another atypical *Redbook* novel: the subject is divorce; the main characters are not young but are in their forties; the wife and mother is an outrageously vicious, scheming, and hypocritical prude; the author's explanation of her behavior is a frank condemnation of the Victorian view of sex and love; and the ending is not happy. The story is, in essence, an unflinching delineation of a "Mom" in action in Middle America.

The vital ingredient in *No Scandal!* is the portrait of Pauline Windon. In all of Wylie's stories there is no more perfect specimen of the American Mom: the ignorant, self-righteous, selfish, domineering, unscrupulous, sexually frigid American middle-class, middle-aged woman, the "human harrow," the kind who produces neurotic sons and sends "inhibited daughters into unstable marriages." In the novel Wylie lists her methods of getting her own way, which include "blackmail, theft, deceit, intimidation, forgery, phony propaganda, censorship, extortion, and torture," whichever is applicable. And, since she is virtually unstoppable, this monstrous matriarch is "responsible, perhaps, for more disaster, more real sin and misery, than any other aspect of the scene around her."

Wylie quite wisely made Pauline a type character. He could have added other traits that would have made her an individual rather than a representative of a class—but that would have obscured his point: Pauline is not an isolated individual with peculiar unpleasant faults; she is, instead, merely one of a legion of demons in female form who have usurped control of contemporary America and completely perverted the ideas and ideals of women and men alike. As Wylie clearly demonstrates, Pauline could not possibly act as she does if she were not supported by the rest of society, which is made up of women who, like herself, hate sex but use it to their own unholy advantage, and of men who have been made so guilty about their sexual needs that they never question the doctrine that the woman is always right because she is "pure." It is, of course, the male minister and the male doctor who represent society's views in *No Scandal!* They try to make Jim surrender to his wife, and it is the doctor who gives Pauline his support, as a man of science and medicine, for her decision to bar Jim from her bed because sex makes her nervous.

Although Wylie is fond of editorializing, he shrewdly allows Pauline's own words to make the point of his novel for him; and nowhere is it more evident than in the mother's advice to her daughter on how to achieve a perfect marriage. First of all, a man's sexual desires must be curbed: "A man has his natural vulgarities and indecencies—but a woman has character with which to meet them." Since marriage is worthwhile only "if *you* make all the choices," the woman must use any tactics necessary to ensure her control. One useful method is to shame him in public: "a man has two weak points—his vanity and his tenderness. When things fail to go as they should, you can score with either one."

The woman, Pauline warns, must resist the temptation to use these strategems until after the marriage; then, of course, the man is helpless; he will do anything to escape nagging or to obtain her sexual favors, and he will never turn to other women because he knows that a divorce will ruin him financially and socially. Pauline's doctrines inevitably emerge from her daughter's mouth, as evidenced in the girl's response to her father when he tries to explain why he can no longer continue in a loveless marriage: she advises him not to give her that "Freudian business" and adds, "I expect you've been to too many stag smokers lately, or something." Beth has learned well her mother's lesson on how to destroy a man.

VIII   *The Crunch and Des Stories*

In March, 1940, the *Saturday Evening Post* published a short story, "Widow Voyage," about two Miami charterboat men, Crunch Adams and Desperate Smith, who earn their living by taking people deep-sea fishing on their boat, the *Poseidon*. Philip Wylie was once more seeking for a special kind of literary gold mine—a series that would "catch on." Wylie had been looking for a good idea for a series of stories for ten years, but the closest he had ever come was a group of tales about "The Wild Wallaces," which had succumbed after seven undistinguished pieces had been printed in *Redbook* in 1931.

Ironically, Wylie's opportunity had been in front of him —literally—for ten years. In 1929, he had visited Miami for the first time; he had wintered there frequently in the 1930s; and in 1937 he had become a permanent resident when doctors prescribed a gentle climate to aid his recovery from his Russia-induced illness. He had been an avid fisherman since the age of nine, and by 1930 he had found a new thrill in battling sea monsters in the Gulf Stream, in hanging on desperately to the heavy rod and reel of the deep-sea fishers. He had soon absorbed all of the lore of the sport (he later claimed that he made only one factual error in all of his Crunch and Des stories), and, even more important, he had learned to love the sea in all its moods, colors, and power.

He had occasionally used fishing in stories, but it took a specific event to produce his brainstorm. In 1939, two of his friends, Harold Schmitt and John Smedburg, who wanted to have their own charter boat, raised and reconditioned a burned out hull on their own time and with great effort. Wylie wrote a fictionalized version of the triumph of the hard working boatmen: Crunch was a composite figure, based in part on Schmitt, who had been a Golden Gloves heavyweight champion, and in part on another boatman, Mel Fleeson, while Des bore some resemblance to John Smedburg. When Wylie sent the story to the *Saturday Evening Post*, he noted on the manuscript that he could write more if that one "caught on."

His success was complete. He now became nationally famous instead of fairly well known. The Crunch and Des series was, according to Wylie, the most popular one ever printed in the *Post;* in all, fifty-nine tales were published, and seven of them were thirty-thousand-word novelettes. The last appeared in 1959; at least forty others, according to Wylie's estimates, were written but not published. The stories were quickly reprinted in hard cover book form in *The Big Ones Get Away* (1940), *Salt Water Daffy* (1941), *Fish and Tin Fish* (1944), *Crunch and Des* (1948), *The Best of Crunch and Des* (1954), and *Treasure Cruise* (1956)—not to mention paperback editions and a volume, *Selected Short Stories of*

Philip Wylie, published by the armed services. Collections of stories usually sell poorly, but Wylie's public bought over 511,000 copies.

The obvious explanation of this publishing phenomenon is that readers found in the stories exactly what they liked: fast moving, clearly presented action; evocative description of locale; a good bit of humor and sentiment; and a suspenseful plot with a happy ending. Most important, the hero acted out their fantasies, and he was a muscular, independent, hard working, self-reliant, well-intentioned, completely honest, all-around "nice guy" with whom anyone could identify—no matter how much the reader himself might be lacking in these qualities. And to aid Crunch are his beautiful but sometimes critical wife, Sari, and the loyal, steady, silent, equally hard working best friend, Des, whose darkest secret is his real name, which he has revealed to only one other living person.

But the best part of the fantasy is the villains and what happens to them. They are always big, violent bullies who are skilled in deceit and subterfuge, the sort of rotten people who go through life asking for a good beating—and that is precisely what Crunch gives them. In short, the world which Wylie creates is a beautiful one in which good triumphs, where evil is a simple thing and focused in one tangible being that can be faced and demolished, where the old-fashioned moral standards are clear and obvious and the man who practices them wins and the bad guy runs away into the dusk.

The Crunch and Des stories, despite their deliberate appeal to popular taste, should not be dismissed as "mere escape fiction." To the contrary, the best of them rank first among Wylie's pieces of short fiction. Though the secondary characters are usually one-trait personalities designed for a particular plot, there is nothing shadowy about Crunch, Des, and Sari, who are made to come alive by the lines of dialogue they speak. Nearly every story employs the same basic plot: a person with a problem or dilemma takes a voyage on the *Poseidon* and, in the course of the fishing experience, resolves the situation. Nevertheless, each new tale has a particular freshness and originality. They achieve this effect because Wylie used variations on two basic parallel plots rather than one; the first involves a character's conflicts with other people, and the other deals with the struggle between a person and a fish. Wylie had no problem in devising the former kind, which are usually based on a love triangle. As for the second, he knew countless true and amazing stories about deep-sea fishing and had only to choose those which would seem probable when put into print.

His greatest achievement—and the ultimate reason for the believability of even the most improbable plots—is the setting in which they occur. Wylie placed his action in an extraordinarily real world—a trick he had used earlier in fantasies like *Gladiator*. Every aspect of the fishing boats, the gear, and the methodology of the hunt is carefully detailed. And, always present in the background, there is the sea itself, described in images of sight, touch, and sound that burn themselves into the consciousness and then the memory.

Having impressed both the public and the publishers with his expertise on deep-sea fishing, Wylie was in demand to produce additional material. He found it easy to place a large number of articles on the subject; there are nearly as many as there are Crunch and Des stories. The best of these were reprinted in *Denizens of the Deep* (1953), which sold 92,196 copies. There were other sea stories in *Argosy*, which also printed two of the Crunch and Des stories.

The greatest potential bonanza appeared in 1956, when the National Broadcasting Company announced a television series starring Forrest Tucker, Sandy Kenyon, and Joanne Bays as Crunch, Des, and Sari. The filming was done on Darrel's Island near Bermuda with Wylie on hand as consultant. The plans were to use film clips from the Pathe News library to supplement the movies being made with the cast.[5] Wylie saw that the producers were making all kinds of technical errors and mistakes about the sport; he warned them that the nearly forty million people who fished would know at once that a poor job had been done. They ignored him, because they believed that no one would notice. Thirty-nine episodes were filmed at a cost of over a million dollars. As Wylie had prophesied, the potential sponsors were not fooled: they looked at the first three or four pilot films and walked out. The National Broadcasting Company never was able to sell the series and had to syndicate it. As Wylie sadly said, "You can never tell movie or television people how to do something right."

IX *The Death of an Illusion*

An April Afternoon, published in October, 1938, is a tragically flawed masterpiece. The first eighteen of the twenty chapters are easily equal to the best work Wylie ever produced; they are nearly perfect in plotting and characterization, unprecedented in psychological insights, and overwhelmingly beautiful in prose style and evocation of mood—a slow-paced and gentle meditation on the moral ambiguities of modern life and the saddening errors that are so much a part of the human condition. To this extraordinary work, Wylie inexplicably added two chapters of an entirely different nature. In them he rushes events to wholly improbable conclusions, employs coincidences and a *deus ex machina* to provide an entirely unwarranted happy ending, and violates every known concept of unity by introducing a laughably melodramatic account of the heroic death of the narrator's father years earlier during a volcanic eruption on a South Sea island. The only word capable of describing this sacrilege committed against the rest of the book is Wylie's favorite: it's an "outrage." Fortunately, the contents of the preceding sections of the novel, which includes an important development in Wylie's thinking, more than justify a close look at it.

An April Afternoon was written because Wylie once again wanted to address himself to the problem of finding a satisfactory code for behavior in the contemporary world. In his preceding novels, he had shown increasing disillusionment with the efficacy of the New Morality. In *Too Much of Everything*, he had come close to rejecting it entirely, when the elder Bentlan finally concludes that the concept of complete freedom from ethical rules and restraints is utter foolishness. Now Wylie set out in *An April Afternoon* to see whether Bentlan's proposed formula—freedom with *self*-restraint—would work.

To give his theory a fair test, Wylie invented the Sheffields of Connecticut, a family of sensitive, rational, and intelligent persons of the upper social ranks—a group of people who live by the very liberal "Sheffield code," which says that "the only 'Thou shalt not' is 'Thou shalt not.' But every privilege carries its own responsibility." This maxim, as enunciated by the father, has worked well: the four children are living responsible and useful lives, and minor ethical crises have been surmounted with reasonableness, open-mindedness, and tolerance for the rights of others. Then Wylie introduces a major challenge to the family's ability to cope with moral dilemmas: the mother, beset by fear of middle age and a longing for romance, runs away with a lover. The family's reaction is condemnation and unforgiving anger, the kind of behavior that supposedly "went out" with the Victorians.

Why had the mother acted as if the Sheffield code had advocated hedonism instead of responsible rational behavior? Why did her husband display all the signs of that outdated emotion, sexual jealousy? Why were her grown children intent on punishing her, even when she admitted her error and wanted to return home?

Wylie, drawing upon his recent and extensive exposure to the basic concepts of Jungian psychology, has a simple but stunning answer: the code on which his characters had relied could not work when severely tested because it disregarded the fact that man is a creature whose actions are dominated by his feelings and his instinctual nature. This reality, of which the Sheffields had been ignorant, rendered inoperative all three of the premises on which was based their moral system, in which freedom to make one's own decisions would be counterbalanced by the self-restraint that would ensure responsible behavior.

The first premise is that rational people can be honest with themselves about their desires and motives. The truth, unfortunately, is that it is impossible to think objectively about feelings or situations involving one's feelings, especially when one is having those emotions or even much later (an insight Wylie had received in the analyst's office). Thus, if one cannot obtain sound data on which to base a decision, his power to make correct choices cannot be trusted. So much for "situational ethics"!

The second premise is that, after a person is aware of what his feelings are, he will be able to impose the control of reason on them. The truth is that rational behavior is possible only if one takes into account the overwhelmingly powerful emotional nature of one's self and others and makes one's plans accordingly. Even then, logical actions may be impossible.

The third faulty premise is closely related to the others. The reformers who cast out the rules of the Victorians argued erroneously that moral codes were only cultural in origin—mere attitudes and not expressions of universal truths. They failed to distinguish between the moral laws which *were* merely attitudes and those which are solemn warnings against violating what the narrator calls "racial concepts"—those deeply held convictions about personal, sexual, and family relationships which are perhaps instinctive. The basic laws of human nature cannot be altered or evaded by a "sophisticated" or worldly attitude. What the Victorians had surrounded with ridiculous claptrap and superstition, the moderns had overlooked entirely—and with equally disastrous results. Thus the Sheffields had been trained to believe that they could accept calmly those situations which are, in actuality, intolerable to human beings; it is not surprising that they failed.

When Wylie had completed *An April Afternoon*, he had effected the destruction of one of the myths that had obscured the thinking of his generation. The next step was for him to try to arrive at a correct understanding of man's nature, for only then could he reach any valid conclusions about the kind of ethical system which was required for human guidance. That task would take him the rest of his life and, on the way, would produce *Vipers, An Essay on Morals,* and, finally, *The Magic Animal.*

In emphasizing the philosophical content of *An April Afternoon,* we should not overlook its virtues as literature, which are many. One is the skill with which Wylie created Frankie, his first-person narrator, through whose mind we see the disintegration of the Sheffields' supposedly rational world. This young man is admirably suited for his role because he is, in effect, an "outsider," not only because he is an adopted child but also because of his psychological makeup. Like Wylie, he had been bedridden with a serious illness during childhood and had become withdrawn and introspective: now, as an adult, it is his fate always to see the members of any group and even himself with a strange detachment and objectivity. Having spent years living within his own mind, he is always conscious of the functioning of his own mental processes and thus extremely sensitive to those of others.

Watching events unfold in *An April Afternoon* is an extraordinary experience, for the narrator is a poet as well as a highly analytical being. Everything he observes is described with acutely observed detail and is conveyed in fresh and imaginative diction that is full of compelling figurative language and images. Often the story moves on a non-verbal level through moods and shifts of feeling that are evoked or suggested by the seasons, the time of day, or the color of the landscape—and thus reminds us of Virginia Woolf's *Mrs. Dalloway.* And, throughout the novel, we are constantly aware of the personality of Frankie, the lonely spectator of life, a man compassionate and forgiving, entranced by the melancholy nature of existence, too aware of life's futility to be able to act in his own behalf or even to bear a grudge. There is no character like him anywhere in Wylie's books, and he is one of his most unforgettable creations.

In view of these and other excellent qualities, we can only regret that Wylie, perhaps anticipating that no one would pay much attention to either his ideas or his purely literary achievements, chose ludicrous melodrama as the easiest way to conclude his book instead of writing the appropriate and honest ending which the novel so richly deserves.

CHAPTER 6

The War Years

A S early as 1938 Wylie had stated in *An April Afternoon* that the Spanish Civil War was the first engagement in a world war that would quickly engulf the United States. Not many Americans shared that view, and most were openly hostile to such "war mongering," but Wylie continued to write about the need for military preparedness. This theme appeared in *The Army Way*, composed at the request of William Muir, an army "buff" from a military family. A description of what the new draftees of 1940 could expect in the training camps, it stresses the need for the sacrifice of personal liberty in the cause of freedom for the nation. Wylie would repeat that message endlessly in articles, stories, pamphlets, speeches, and even his books of the desperate years ahead.

I The Other Horseman

Wylie's support of the Stop Hitler Movement led him, in the fall of 1941, to write a propaganda novel aimed at the isolationist policies of the America First Committees and at the anti-war sentiment of the Midwest. The main character of *The Other Horseman* is Jimmie Bailey, an American research chemist who returns to his native Midwest in 1941 after six years in England, where he had been an inventor of secret weapons during the Blitz. He has been assigned by the United States government to continue his work in the chemical plant of Willie Corinth; he finds that he has an additional task—to carry the truth about Hitler to his family and to other isolationists.

The plot, therefore, is largely a series of debates for and against intervention by the United States. Wylie's efforts were entirely wasted because the book was not published until July, 1942, long after Pearl Harbor, when its main issue had become academic.

Furthermore, its literary merits are few because the one-trait characters are merely spokesmen for the opposing points of view and because the events in the novel are predictable illustrations of the theme. Among its few merits are satirical portraits of the American Mom and the Republican businessman. Also, in Willie Corinth's monologues are many of the Jungian theories that are the philosophical basis of the forthcoming *Generation of Vipers*. However, since most of these ideas are merely stated but not dramatized or explained, many readers will find them hard to grasp.

II   *The Unchained Satirist*

Wylie's next book, *Generation of Vipers*, was written in a savage explosion of energy. Returning to Miami from Washington, D.C., early in 1942, he was seething with rage. Despite the war, most of his fellow Americans were showing their usual selfishness and unwillingness to make any sacrifices for the cause of freedom. Especially irritating to him were the liberal intellectuals in the government who had rejected his plans to publicize the Bataan Death March and other atrocities in order to mobilize public support of the war. On May 12, at Ricky Wylie's suggestion, Philip sat down at his typewriter to put on paper his opinions on the moral and spiritual condition of contemporary America—mostly to relieve his feelings and with little thought of trying to get them published. In a mere fifty-four days he hammered out an amazing one hundred twenty-five thousand words in a state of inspiration so continuous and intense that hardly a word needed changing when he decided to submit the manuscript to Farrar and Rinehart. Once more, as when he had written *Finnley Wren*, personal frustration had produced the anger that generated, in turn, the psychic energy needed to produce a masterpiece.

The elaborate subtitle, reminiscent of that of *Finnley Wren*, is a good summation of the contents and method of *Vipers:* "A Survey of Moral Want and a Philosophical Discourse Suitable Only for the Strong—a Study of American Types and Archetypes and a Signpost on the Two Thoroughfares of Men: *The Via Dolorosa* and the *Descensus Averno*—Together with Sundry Preachments, Epithets . . . Moodal Adventures . . . Political Impertinences . . . Allegories . . . Aspirations . . . Visions and Jokes—as well as Certain Homely Hints for the Care of the Human Soul." If nothing else, this statement establishes the tone of the book to follow, a quality Wylie described to me in 1970 as "very loud." The term, "Preachments," is especially apt, for the book is a sermon—a hellfire and brimstone call for repentance and belief in a new doctrine, the gospel according to Jung.

Vipers contains a foreword, a preface, a second preface, and eighteen essays. The original edition begins with a one-page address to the reader entitled "You Bought the War." Interventionists and isolationists, voters and non-voters alike, are reminded that this war is the price of freedom and that it was caused by men who wanted to seize the world and by other men who waited too long to pay the price for peace—who forgot that only a vigilant defense of freedom for all can prevent war. The aim of *Vipers* is to examine these causes so that a third war may be prevented.

"Preface," an eleven-page explanation of how *Vipers* came to be written, was dropped after 1954, when Wylie composed an updated introduction. Nevertheless, it is well worth reading for its account of the author's attempts over the years to obtain a hearing for his prophecies and warnings about Germany and for its expression of his inescapable need to write a book that would be something besides entertainment, some real contribution to knowledge. It is also the best (and probably only) account of his fifteen-year search for a meaning in life—"Wylie's wilderness period." At last, he says, he turned to a thorough study of psychology and discovered the concept of "subjective reality," the fact that "the psyche operates in many ways besides those of verbalized logic and the logic of mathematics." He became convinced that in this area of research lies the possibility of real self-knowledge, the discovery of a valid moral system, and thus true fulfillment. He came to realize that he now understood the "collective attitudes" of mankind and thus the real causes—and a cure—for such evils as war and economic disruptions; as a result, he now had a purpose for his life—the education of mankind into a new religion through his writings.

The second preface, "Directions for Reading This Book" (also dropped in 1954), explains that we can read straight through or begin with any chapter because the book has a single theme. It is "the affirmative of the debate: 'Resolved, that Americans have lost their moral sensibilities by living too objectively and with too little subjective awareness.'" Wylie then defends his "frequent use of literary devices intended to affect the feelings, by a deliberate injection of libido into values," on the grounds that *Vipers* is a sermon, a

genre in which such methods are legitimate "routes to realities."
He warns, however, that his three discussions of three psychological
laws, which are of a "textbook nature," do require thorough understanding and mastery; otherwise, the book will be only "one vast
gripe." He then outlines the whole book briefly in order to show its
form and direction.

The opening chapter, "Catastrophe, Christ, and Chemistry,"
asserts that both Christianity and science have failed to solve mankind's dilemmas and have, instead, increased them. Christianity has
never restrained men from barbarism; it has lost sight of its few
valid discoveries and clung desperately instead to its rituals and
superstitions; and, in present day America, it has succumbed to the
attacks of science and reason. Science too has failed: in limiting
itself only to observable physical phenomena and denying the existence of the subjective reality of the human psyche, it has produced a vacuum in the spirit of man; there has been no attempt to
apply the search for truth to man's inner nature. The only salvation
of man must come through "a general increase in the consciousness
of man" in the area of self-knowledge and real honesty.

The following chapters are designed to convince the reader that
so-called modern civilized men are really "still medieval—cruel
bumpkins and dancing savages," for only when people are convinced of the nature of the problem will they possess either the will
or the means to cope with it. With this intention firmly in mind,
Wylie presents in "Subjective Feudalism" a description of America
in 1940 (a "brutal and degraded era") as it might appear in a book
by an historian in the distant future.

After this masterpiece of horror, Wylie presents in "A Psychology
Lesson, a Study, and a Sermon" an explication of the theories of Dr.
Carl Jung concerning man's instincts and the concept of the
"archetypes" in the universal myths of mankind. Wylie then argues
that Christianity lost its function as a "repository of instincts" when
it substituted "dogmatic perfectionism" (standards of behavior impossible for people to achieve) for growth *towards* virtue and laid
claim to magical methods of achieving perfection, especially
through "a system of vicarious punishment" and atonement by
Christ for men's sins. Wylie asserts that there is no hope for man
until he accepts himself for what he is, a constant battleground, and
gives up the hope of instant cures.

Chapter V, "A Specimen American Myth," examines the perversion of the Cinderella legend by modern Americans. Originally, the

story symbolized the possibility of finding a worthy and virtuous Cinderella in an unlikely locale. But now the incentive to merit a reward for virtue is replaced with the idea that everyone, especially the female, automatically is entitled to "the good life," which has come to mean material goods only; the emphasis is on the reward, not the struggle to be the best.

Chapter VI, "A Specimen American Attitude," explores the hypocrisy of—and the danger in—the conception held in this country of man's sexual nature. Current mores refuse to recognize the sexual instinct as a "giant compulsion" constantly manifesting itself. Wylie feels that "a naturalistic attitude toward sex will do away with much of our insanity and neurosis," promote better marriages, lessen the hostility between the sexes, and remove the immense guilt feelings which produce harsh public reaction and retribution against sexual offenders, particularly homosexuals.

Chapter VII, "A Specimen American Institution," dissects the American school, which he calls "the instrument of stupidity and lies." It instills "facts" (especially about American history, political geography, and economics) which are lies, and it gives no instruction in how to think. Wylie directs special criticism toward the teaching of reading and the art of communication—there are, he says, not a million adults who are capable of understanding the ideas in *Vipers*.

Chapter VIII, "Common Man: The Hero's Backside," annihilates a cherished American concept—the wonderfulness of the "common man." In actuality, the hero of the American legend is greedy, superstitious, ignorant, untrustworthy, lazy, cruel, politically irresponsible, and thoroughly dishonest. It is the common man who has been responsible for the decline of every civilization which has yet emerged because he cannot resist the chance to profit at the expense of the community.

Chapter IX, "The New Order for Common Man," is an explication of the law of oppositeness: the laws of action and reaction apply to subjective processes as well as to physical ones, and the moral human being must take into account these extreme alterations in emotional sets in order to control his behavior. Wylie then examines anti-Semitism to show that the real reasons for it are subjective and not admitted by the persecutors, who cannot afford to recognize them. The real reason for the anti-Semitism is the need for a scapegoat for our own personal failures. The Jew is a convenient target for common man because some Jews, as a result of the grim

laws of natural selection, are superior in intelligence and craf-
tiness—and common man instinctively tries to destroy anything
really better than he.

Chapter X, "Uncommon Men," which has been frequently
anthologized, is the first of seven pictures of American types—it discusses the scientist, especially the medical doctor. Wylie indicts
him, first, for failing to recognize the subjective or psychological
causes of half of his patients' illnesses. Furthermore, doctors make
no attempt at preventive medicine and, in fact, undermine all efforts to establish health-insurance programs or to create public
health services in slums because they fear a loss of income.

Chapter XI, "Common Women," is the most widely read and
anthologized section of *Vipers*, the definitive picture of "Mom"
which gave that noun and "Momism" to the language. Mom is
what Cinderella becomes after marriage—a self-centered, completely useless creature freed of all work by machines and by the notion of men that the woman deserves worship, money, and power
because she is a female; an idle middle-aged harpy who displays her
self-serving voracity and incredible stupidity by interfering in
politics, law, religion, education, art, and science, consistently
defeating all attempts at reform or enlightenment.

In Chapter XII, "Businessmen," Wylie attacks the most
respected and sacred profession in modern America—business. He
attributes its exalted status to Mom, whose materialism makes it impossible for her to appreciate any male profession unless it makes
money; naturally, she is also the chief defender of the chief
purveyor of everything she cares about. Wylie then moves on to the
economists, the allies of the businessmen: they assert that man is an
economic animal and that all history can be explained by economic
causes. They should, instead, examine the causes of economics,
which lie in man's subjective nature.

In Chapter XIII, "Statesmen," Wylie declares that statesmen
throughout history have been parties to immorality in international
dealings, the expansionist goals of business, and the precipitation of
violence to achieve their goals. In Chapter XIV, "Professors," Wylie
rebukes college teachers for continuing to present traditional
courses that have no usefulness, for departmentalizing knowledge,
for not teaching wisdom, and for instilling the nonsense of such
pseudo-sciences as sociology and economics into their students, who
then try to reform the world with their Left-wing nonsense.

Chapter XV, "Congressmen—with a Footnote on Mecca," affirms that the stupidity, dishonesty, greed, and incompetence of the elected officials are, in fact, representative of the people who send them to Washington. As a result, democracy may succumb to dictatorship because the people have abused liberty and handed over their power to scoundrels.

Chapter XVI, "Military Men," includes much more than denunciations of the nation's military caste. War, after all, is not caused by soldiers, but by the failure of a nation to cope with the realities of man's subjective nature. Indeed, there will always be wars until mankind abandons scientific materialism and learns to deal honestly with itself. Furthermore, the morale of the ordinary American soldier, who must fight the war, is very low because he believes in no values except the material ones which his society has given him. Soldiers are further handicapped by their own ideology, which stresses blind obedience and not the creative individualism and employment of new weapons and strategies which win wars.

In Chapter XVII, "The Man on the Cross," Wylie gives his interpretation of the teachings of Jesus of Nazareth. "The one, great positive idea which Christ repeatedly tried to express was the thought that no individual human being could know himself unless his inner honesty was complete: the peace he talked of was inner peace, and he said so, always. The way to it was through truth and through the abandonment of preoccupation with temporal matters . . . . No man, according to Christ, could know himself unless he knew all the negative and inferior aspects of himself . . . . A man . . . who did not know himself could not in any way trust what he thought about other men or the world." Thus the path to salvation lay in the difficult and painful effort to achieve "private integrity."

In Chapter XVIII, "Conclusion," Wylie restates his thesis, "if we want a better world, we will have to be better people," and then describes the millenium that is possible. An America which does not confuse "goods" with goodness, which strives "to become more conscious of reality" and puts "obligations to others" ahead of its own ambitions, which encourages the "*valid* feelings and ideas in minorities," which recognizes "the right to all information as the route to all understanding and judgement" (in other words, the freedom to know), and which rejects "economic panaceas and social nostrums" in favor of the education of common man in idealism and spiritual and psychic realities—this America will fulfill its destiny as the leader and savior of all of mankind.

When Farrar and Rinehart brought out *Vipers* in January, 1943, Wylie thought that the press run of four thousand copies was too large: he was aware that books of essays don't move well, and his subject, he knew, would hardly be popular or welcome. Few periodicals reviewed it, and most of the critical reactions were unenthusiastic. Yet, on the Sunday evening before the official publication, Walter Winchell, Wylie's long-time ally in the Stop Hitler movement, praised it extravagantly on his radio program. Astonishingly, the first printing of *Vipers* was sold out in a week, and the demand increased. Word-of-mouth advertising soon made it one of those "underground classics" that seemingly make their way without the customary boosts from advertising copy or friendly reviews.

By 1954, four years before the first paperback edition appeared, *Vipers* had sold one hundred eighty thousand copies and was still averaging five thousand annually; in fact, Wylie had never permitted it to be printed in a cheaper edition because the hard cover sales had held up so incredibly well. Thus, with a book which he had expected to be a slow seller Wylie achieved an amazingly large readership, a fame that was far wider even than that of the creator of Crunch and Des, and a role he played ever afterward—that of seer, prophet, and scourge-bearer of the Western World.

Vipers became a legend in its own time (Wylie estimated that he had received over sixty thousand letters from readers, ninety-five percent of them favorable)—and for three very good reasons. One was the absolute fearlessness with which Wylie attacked American types and institutions that had browbeaten nearly everyone else into timid silence. His audacity immediately made him the hero of those who shared his views but lacked the courage to air them. Another reason was the evident truthfulness of what he was saying. He had opened his readers' eyes to facts that should have been self-evident, and never again would Cinderella, Mom, money-hungry doctors, and the rest of his targets be able to command the unthinking respect of those whom they had fooled for so long. But the most important cause for the notoriety of *Vipers* was the manner in which Wylie had expressed himself. His was not a calmly reasoned indictment; it was a tirade of unrestrained ferocity, a stream of invective poured forth without qualification or equivocation and uninhibited by the conventions of propriety, by pity for his victims, or even by the rules of fair play.

But though some may have thought that Wylie had been carried away by his own fury, he was, in fact, quite conscious of what he was doing—he was making a calculated assault on the emotions of his readers in order to achieve an aim which sweet reasonableness could not, namely to convert them to views that were antithetical to those they had held for a lifetime. His two favorite—and most devastating—devices are "name-calling" and "card-stacking" of examples. The apt and crushing epithet, he knew, would do more than express his own anger and contempt: his example would cause others to discover within themselves their own suppressed or even unsuspected feelings of hostility. Moreover, by subjecting his targets to ridicule and scorn, he would be demonstrating that they were not omnipotent but, instead, vulnerable to criticism and attack. His choice of the most horrendous examples possible and his delineation of the most sickening, blood-chilling, nauseating, or terrifying details are equally effective in producing an emotional response in that they bring to readers an experience of reality that statistics and bland or "balanced" generalizations can never elicit. It is not surprising that textbooks on argumentation often cite passages from *Vipers* as illustrations of the art in one of its most extraordinary forms.

Because of the controversy *Vipers* had aroused, it became perhaps the best-known book of its time, and Wylie became a prophet with honor—or, at least, notoriety. For the rest of his life, he was called upon to produce the kind of articles which editors had rejected in earlier years. Apparently, readers might object to his views, but they wanted to hear them, too. *Cosmopolitan* elicited essays on "What's Wrong with Women's Clothes?," "What's Wrong with Colleges for Women?," "What's Wrong with Youthfulness?," "What's Wrong with State Patriotism?," and "Some Plain Talk for Brides and Grooms." He wrote a number of "spin offs" on Momism like "Mom's to Blame," "What's Happened to 'Mom'?," and "Pop Is a Moral Slacker." A series by him appeared in various Sunday supplements, he had for a time a syndicated newspaper column, and he even on occasion appeared in *Reader's Digest* (but in his milder manner). Where Crunch and Des had brought minor intrusions on Wylie's privacy, he now faced the problem of all American celebrities—how to keep the tourists from trampling his flowerbeds. He even found himself being impersonated by confidence men of various types—ranging from bad check artists to would-be seducers of female fans of his book.[1]

The two most frequent questions aimed at him were "Do you

hate women?" and "Are you serious?" In vain he protested in articles and interviews that he *loved* women and hated only those who
disgraced their sex; without success he protested that "Common
Women" was only one chapter of eighteen. To the second question,
he always replied, "Lord, yes!" But readers often refused to believe
that sincerity of purpose was compatible with humor, especially
what Wylie called "gallows humor." Slowly he realized that too
many people saw *Vipers* as a half-serious gripe and had missed the
really important ideas in it. With that recognition was born the
resolve to write a book of ideas that would not be misunderstood.
When it appeared, in 1947, it was called *An Essay on Morals;* it will
be discussed in Chapter 7.

III Night Unto Night: *The Gothic in Florida*

In September, 1944, Farrar and Rinehart brought out *Night Unto
Night,* Wylie's first important work in nearly two years and one
which in various editions eventually sold an amazing 424,280
copies. In his preface Wylie discussed the origin of the book. A year
and a half earlier (apparently in March, 1943), while at the
Washington home of his friend, Milton MacKaye, Wylie had been
talking about how Americans avoid any thought or contemplation
of death. The conversation had then turned to ghosts and immortality, and especially to Wylie's latest conviction, based on a
Jungian idea, that consciousness survived the physical death of the
body through a reunion with a fundamental consciousness that ex-
isted beyond time and space as we know of them. Mrs. MacKaye,
herself a writer, "suggested that my argument had made the theme
for a novel; forthwith she outlined its principal characters, its setting, and its central problem . . . . I thought about that kernel of
commencement for a month or two—and spent the best part of a
year writing this book."

Though Wylie wanted to prove himself as a polemicist and artist,
his main reason for writing this novel was to deal with his own
private demon—his obsession with and fear of death, which had
been reawakened by the spectacle of mass slaughter all over the
planet. Even a man not given to introspection might, in such times,
dwell on mortality; and Wylie found himself wondering often how
mankind could bear to live with the insistent knowledge of the inevitability of the end of life. Since even the Crunch and Des stories
reflected a preoccupation with death in this same period, it is likely

that he would have written a book like *Night Unto Night* even without the initial impulse given by his evening at the MacKaye's.

The novel centers on the experiences of two people, Ann Gracey and John Galen, in the spring, summer, and fall of 1942. In Part I, "The Beach," Ann is staying in the old Gracey house while her husband, Bill, serves on a submarine chaser based at Miami Beach; one evening she undergoes a ghastly experience when the tide reaches an unusual height and brings in a life raft with five machine-gunned corpses. With the courage of her New England upbringing, she tows it ashore and discovers that the men are members of Bill's crew. Bill's body is never found, and she begins the painful experience of loss and anguish. Later, while alone in the house, she hears Bill call her name and say, "It's here."

In Part II, "The Men," John, a brilliant college teacher, researcher in biology, and successful businessman, learns, when he attempts to enlist in the Air Corps, that he has inherited epileptic tendencies that may become progressively worse. On the advice of Johann Altheim, his friend and analyst, he takes a vacation in Florida; while looking for a house to rent, he meets Ann just as she is fleeing her haunted home. He rents the house, and, later, sustains a fall down the stairs, perhaps caused by a spectral push.

In the longest section, "The Dead," John meets Henry Maddox, a doctor who treats his badly twisted ankle, and his date, Gail Chapman, the promiscuous and lovely sister of Ann. Maddox tells John of the fate of Paul Gracey, who had died in the house and whose body had not been discovered until devoured by rats and insects. Meanwhile, Ann, unable to find surcease of sorrow in religion or in the loneliness of her hotel room, takes a job managing a small group of rental cottages near the Gracey house and begins nightly vigils, during which she hopes to encounter Bill's spirit again. Entering the house during John's absence, she again hears the voice, which assures her that he is all right, repeats that "it's here," admonishes her to "be you," and says goodbye.

In the final division, "The Tide," John discovers that his condition, as he had feared, is terminal; and the story follows him in his last days. Johann Altheim, who flies to Florida to be with his friend, gives his blessing to John's marriage with Ann. The psychiatrist then investigates the meaning of the message from the dead, locates a letter which Bill had once received in which Gail is accused of murdering her husband and infant son, and then uses his skill as an analyst to prove to Gail that she was not really responsible for the deaths. The house is destroyed by fire during a hurricane, and, not long after, John dies in a moment of perfect awareness of the eternal—a "becalmed ecstasy—this crystallized forever."

The preceding summation may give the false impression that the plot is very important in *Night Unto Night*. Actually, it serves mainly as a means of bringing characters together for discussions or debates, of providing occasions for inserting pieces of writing done by the characters themselves, or of setting in motion long passages of introspective internal monologues. Only the last section, in which Wylie introduces the mysterious letter about Gail in a final effort to prove that ghosts do exist, is heavily plotted; and this unconvincing part, which too much resembles the end of a murder mystery, is the major defect in the novel. The best sections of the book are without plot; they are those in which the action is internal, as in Ann's painful search for happiness in memories of the past or in John's attempts to subdue the fear of death that obliterates the outside world and makes dying the lonely business that it is.

The quality of the writing in *Night Unto Night*, which, for sustained brilliance, is unrivaled in his books, attests to the unusual amount of time spent on the novel and to Wylie's professional competence. The extraordinarily detailed and evocative descriptions of settings, and especially those of the climate and physical characteristics of southern Florida, provide the solidly real backgrounds which are essential in works about the supernatural if the reader is to be persuaded to accept the events as true. Moreover, each major character, especially when his words and thoughts are quoted at length, is brought to life because he has his own style, one that is so carefully individualized that there is never any doubt about whose words they are. One factor that explains the excellence of the style is Wylie's choice for the novel of a loose structure that permitted him to deal with individual sections fully instead of sacrificing them to the demands of a plot. For example, by this means he was able to spend over seven thousand words to evoke the full horror and strangeness of the unforgettable opening scene, in which Ann recovers the corpses from the sea. That passage, incidentally, was written in one sustained burst of excitement in Rushford, New York; but, interrupted by personal affairs, Wylie was never able to recapture the mood (taped interview with Keefer, August, 1970). This incident thus illustrates the importance of inspiration even to a writer with years of experience.

Two themes dominate *Night Unto Night*. One, presented mostly through a minor character named Mullcup, is the author's denunciations of contemporary America's values. The reader familiar with *Vipers* does not find any change in Wylie's basic premises, but he is not bored by repetition because he soon discovers that quite a few symptoms of contemporary insanity had been overlooked in the earlier book. As we have already indicated, Wylie's main theme in *Night Unto Night* is the nature and meaning of death. The possibility of personal immortality is debated at length by all the major characters; but Wylie, realizing that readers would be wary of believing in the opinions and experiences of an unnerved, grief-torn widow or an epileptic facing his own end, employs Johann Altheim to prove that there is life after death. He introduces Altheim as both a completely honest scientist and—even more important in a case like this—a psychiatrist who knows his own mind so well that it cannot play tricks on him. Obviously, if such a man finds evidence that the supernatural is real, the reader has no choice but to accept the author's belief in the hereafter.

Almost from the beginning, Altheim encounters strange events which he explains as psychic phenomena. For instance, shortly after his arrival, he has a dreadful nightmare about dying in his bed; the next day, when he learns that the previous owner of the house had perished there, he attributes his own experience, not to coincidence or the eeriness of the old house, but to the existence of some "influence" that had given him a dream "with roots in some other reality or somebody else's reality." Later, after learning that Ann "heard" the voice of her dead husband saying, "It's here," he does not even consider the possibility that her emotional state leaves her open to self-deception or hallucinations. Instead, he starts searching the house for "it"; when he finds a letter accusing Gail of murder, he confidently asserts that the existence of the document confirms the reality of Ann's experience. (It is possible that the ghost—or Ann's imagination—had in mind some other antecedent for its pronoun, but Altheim again avoids such likelihoods.)

Like Wylie himself in this period, Altheim has a strong preference for supernatural causes of events. For instance, when someone proposes that the message from the ghost was really Ann's recollection of a telepathic transference of Bill's anxiety to Ann while he was still alive, the psychiatrist refuses to discuss that theory; instead, he asserts that "Nobody can tell you what to think about a transcendental experience. . . ," a statement that reveals a very unscientific belief in the unproved premise that there is such a thing as a transcendental experience. Altheim prefers another explanation of her experience: "perhaps entities—the very arrangement of atoms—produced a delicate emanation—a continual announcement of mere presence."

No doubt there were many readers of *Night Unto Night* who were persuaded by Altheim's findings and interpretations, but, as I have suggested, the psychiatrist is not the reliable analyst which Wylie claimed, nor is his evidence in the least persuasive or logical. Consequently, to me, the whole novel, when examined closely, begins to look like the work of a clever but fallible charlatan. Ironically, in a few years Wylie himself lost all his belief in survival beyond the grave. "I was kidding myself," he told me. "When you are dead, that's it." [2]

IV *Service to the Nation*

By the end of the war years, Wylie had contributed a large amount of his time and writing talent to the war effort at great cost to himself and often with real risk involved. He composed several radio scripts, "The Enemy" and "This Is War—What Can I Do?", and prepared an Air Force manual, *Survival*, which explained how to maintain life while lost at sea in a rubber life raft. While testing the survival gear he had helped design, he and a friend were actually lost track of by an escort vessel for many hours, an experience that formed the basis of "The Shipwreck of Crunch and Des." While serving on the Dade County (Florida) Defense Council, he wrote a Civil Defense manual that was widely reprinted, and he was rewarded by being made an honorary lieutenant-colonel in the Florida National Guard.

Wylie's most dangerous assignment started in April, 1945, when he began flying on training missions in the new B-29 bombers, which were stationed at Wright Field, Dayton, Ohio, in order to prepare a history of the air war against Japan for the Air Force Bureau of Personnel Narratives. Engine fires on the badly designed planes repeatedly tested his courage, and he once escaped death because he had, by chance, not flown with his regular crew, who were blown to bits by an on-board explosion. He left the project when he learned that it was duplication of the work of the regular historians and would probably never be printed.

CHAPTER 7

The Decade of Anxiety
(1945-1955)

WITH the end of World War II and the start of the Atomic Age, Wylie became busier than ever at writing and at new duties for the government. His article, in 1945, "Deliverance or Doom," which explained the absolute necessity for civilian control of atomic energy, drew him into the six-month struggle in Congress to establish the Atomic Energy Commission and led to his becoming a close friend and adviser of Senator Brien McMahon, Chairman of the Special Committee on Atomic Energy. After obtaining a "Q" clearance, Wylie visited as part of his duties the atomic tests in Nevada, prepared a feasible list of imaginative nuclear weapons for the United States Navy, and counseled McMahon to advise Truman to build the hydrogen bomb. From 1949 to 1954 he worked as a special consultant to the Federal Civil Defense Administration, which was preparing for a Russian nuclear attack on this country.

Wylie also devoted time to a favorite project of his own, the Lerner biological research laboratory in Bimini; to book reviewing for the *Saturday Review;* to speeches and prefaces on books about sex education and related matters; to building a splendid new home in Miami; and to caring for his teenage daughter, of whom he finally obtained custody. Somehow he managed to write six books, including the incomparable *Opus 21*, all of which reflect his reaction to contemporary events; dozens of Crunch and Des stories; a multitude of *Viper*-ish articles on American life; a syndicated newspaper column; and a propaganda speech for the *Voice of America*, as well as assorted serials and other pieces of magazine fiction. He also wrote at this time his widely anthologized personal essays, "Science Has Ruined My Supper," "Memorandum on Anti-Semitism," "Safe and Insane," and "Another Modest Proposal," his best work in that genre. Then, at the end of this decade of constant anxiety over the nuclear menace and of incessant overwork, Wylie made a terrible discovery: he had suddenly become an old man who was on the point of emotional collapse.

I   An Essay on Morals

In January, 1947, appeared *An Essay on Morals*, a sixty-thousand-word treatise in which Wylie expanded his explanation of the Jungian theories which had been the philosophical basis of *Generation of Vipers*. Some readers, having noted that *Vipers* contained mostly negative criticism, had urged him to state exactly what he did believe or, as the writer of the dust cover said, "to present his philosophy entire." Wylie may have felt, also, that he had not devoted enough space to make Jung's ideas clear. In any case, in the fall of 1946, he could see a real need for a book about morals: the Atomic Age had begun, and there was every reason to believe that man would destroy himself unless he achieved a sane philosophy by which to guide his actions. As Wylie noted in *An Essay on Morals*, the traditional religions, having been exposed as fraudulent, now seemed to have nothing to say to modern man. Science, being concerned only with objective reality, could offer nothing in the way of ethical advice, which is a matter for the subjective side of man. But Wylie, as he said in his preface, had found an answer—a kind of religion—after years of reading extensively in "philosophy, comparative religion and psychology beyond the point at which doctorates are given." In particular, he seems to have read everything Jung ever wrote. Now the time had come to share his truth; and, as he noted with pride, Jung himself had "expressed his general satisfaction" with the book and its exposition of Jungian ideas.

Chapter One describes the "increasing desperateness" of modern man as he awaits annihilation from atomic bombs. Chapter Two deals with the ways men have reacted to the assertion that they are animals. Some who accept this view believe that man has evolved beyond instinct—and thus may be improved by being placed within the proper social and economic system. Others see man as a creature of such brutal instincts that he must be controlled by force in a totalitarian state. From these two views have resulted the grim failures of Communism and Socialism, on the one hand, and the regimentation of Fascism on the other. The religious majority, insisting that man is not an animal, have obstructed any investigation of his true nature; by refusing to believe that God is a human invention and that "man must take the responsibility alone for looking at himself alone with all the knowledge he has lately gained," they have denied him any chance at dignity, humility, inner peace, and, probably, physical survival as a species.

Chapter Three surveys the failure of scientists to make any significant study of man's instincts and offers the hypothesis that instinct is "engaged, among all men . . . in the concealment of itself" from man because he is compelled to think of himself as divine. In Chapter Four, Wylie points out that every individual recapitulates the stages through which consciousness has evolved—from non-awareness toward nearly total comprehension of itself and the world.

In Chapter Five, Wylie discusses Freud's discoveries concerning the role of man's sexual instincts, which operate in the unconscious mind and help to determine his behavior. Chapter Six offers further proof of the existence of instinct and explains that man chose to suppress his awareness of his instincts in order to avoid accepting his own death as an inescapable reality. Chapter Seven deals with methods of detecting the functioning of the ego in one's self, despite the difficulty of seeing one's self objectively.

Chapter Eight explores the proper use of man's instinctual patterns. Man has always possessed the means to solve his moral problems—the conscience, which is the voice of his instincts; reason is merely a kind of sense, "an orderly perception of the sense impressions." The development of reason attuned to the instincts is slowly evolving in mankind, just as other senses have. In Chapter Nine, Wylie explains why the reorientation of the personality takes courage: "it involves the willingness to sacrifice every old idea the self had of itself," and it brings the individual into conflict with the church, which must suppress the fact that man is an animal or else go out of business. One must also overcome the idea that instincts are "evil" or "sinister."

Wylie then examines the patterns of instinct brought out in three representative types by the exigencies of the Atomic Age. After studying the soldier and the scientist, Wylie, in Chapter Twelve, chooses the clergyman as his target, for he is the representative of the church—the chief obstacle to man's enlightenment and true transcendence. Chapter Thirteen develops Wylie's thesis that there are subjective plagues as well as objective ones—and that the world is currently having neurotic and psychotic epidemics. In fact, every one of man's past civilizations has been so affected since "all

religions and all patriotisms are mental epidemics," easily visible to
outsiders but concealed from the victims, who regard the
questioners as themselves mad.

These two diseases—religion and patriotism—are based on the
need of individuals to feel superior—to other animals and other
people—and are the major disturbers of human affairs when these
people try to establish a status quo based on their own particular
ideas instead of following the demands of instinct. Nowhere is there
a better example of how the suppressing of instincts can destroy
offenders than in sex life in America. The fundamental question
that arises is why people insist on viewing their sexual instinct as
evil and on keeping sex a "national secret" when doing so is
destroying them as individuals, as families, and as a nation. Wylie's
answer is that they are compelled to do so by their egos: to accept
the sex drive as a fundamental instinct is to admit that man is an
animal, and to admit that he is born like an animal is to concede
that he will also die like one. Thus, to stamp out sex in thought,
word, and deed—by whatever means is necessary—is to stamp out
mortality.

Wylie's cure is a sweeping one. He insists on an end to the use of
euphemisms for the sex organs and functions; the establishment of
sex education in the schools; the unimpeded distribution of all kinds
of information on the subject, including the arts and techniques of
love making; and, most important, the abolition of the church's
control over sexual behavior.

In Chapter Fourteen, Wylie, after restating his main points, puts
forward his program to bring about personal and international
peace. Fundamentally, it requires that the individual extend his
awareness of his instincts "through study and introspection and
living" in order to live honestly. In his final chapter, Wylie exhorts
his readers to share both his sense of the present crisis and of the excitement and promise of mankind's future.

An Essay on Morals was a success in spite of itself—but not the
kind Wylie had intended. He made few, if any, converts to Jung (or
so he said in *Opus 21*); and this failure is probably due to the unbelievably obscure expression that makes the book almost incomprehensible. Yet the uproar among the critics over its views on sex
and religion—and the scandal caused by fanatics who destroyed
library copies—made it a celebrated work. Eventually, 61,862
copies of it were sold, and across the country people set
themselves—for their own varied reasons—the task of comprehend-

ing an almost unreadable book. These people carried away one insight—that Puritanical attitudes toward sex must be eradicated and men freed from those shackles on their sanity and happiness. Consequently, a great and lengthy struggle was begun. Censorship of literary work was eventually abolished by court action; laws governing sexual acts between consenting adults were found to be unconstitutional; and in the 1960s the nation had its sexual revolution—with attendant revolting excesses. To say that this change all began with Wylie is to make an assertion that cannot be proved—but who can think that all those copies of *An Essay on Morals* had no impact?

II   Opus 21

Twenty-seven months after *An Essay on Morals* crashed into the public consciousness, Wylie renewed the assault in May, 1949, with *Opus 21*, a great novel and possibly his best book. In it he combined his role as a creator of character, mood, and fictional reality with that of interpreter of Jungian doctrine and, inevitably, satirist and castigator of his fellow Americans. As America sank deeper and deeper into the fears and silence of the Joe McCarthy Era, there was one voice still loudly and abrasively saying exactly what it believed—and, furthermore, it was insisting that its free speech was a right second only to the right to know.

Wylie appears to have had three different and complementary aims while composing *Opus 21*. Although he told me in 1970 that his primary purpose was to write another purely "literary" novel like *Finnley Wren*, the truth is that his overriding concern in this instance was really to make another attempt to promulgate Jungian theory to his readers. He decided to use a fictional character named Philip Wylie as the protagonist and narrator, partly because he had used him as an amusing innovation in *Finnley Wren*, but mostly because he had gotten used to speaking directly to his audience in *Vipers* and in *An Essay on Morals*. A second aim was to tell about an actual experience which he felt might be instructive: his reaction when he had been told back in 1947 that he would probably die of cancer within a few months. In this sense, *Opus 21* is, like *Night Unto Night*, a book about death and its meaning. Third, and perhaps unconsciously, Wylie wanted to show his readers just what he was really like and how he applied his own philosophy to life. He had advocated dealing with one's self with complete honesty; here, he felt, he could show that he was not afraid to tell the world about his weaknesses and his times of confusion, despair, self-pity, and egotism. Perhaps, also unconsciously, he wished to show that he was not a hate-filled misanthropist—or misogynist.

Opus 21 is a unique mixture of fact and fiction. A warning prefaces the story: "Most of the characters in this book are unreal—and that is particularly true of the author . . . . Few of the events recorded here ever took place—exactly." With the exception of Ricky, his wife, Karen, his daughter, and Harold Ober, his agent, no real people or real names were lifted from life. On the other hand, Wylie did draw on some specific persons for parts of certain characters. The high society madam, Hattie Blaine, was a composite of Polly Adler, Lee Francis, and others he had met in his "wilder years." The harlot, Gwen Taylor, with whom Wylie holds intellectual discussions, owes her origins to many such girls whom he had known. Paul Wilson's emotional collapse is based on that of a real person who married a prostitute, could not cope with the resultant stresses, and spent years in a mental institution. The scene in which Paul nearly commits suicide comes in part from Wylie's own experience with a distraught girl who threatened to jump from a window. The Jewish lawyer, Dave Berne, was inspired in part by his friend, Emile Zola Berman, war hero and then a celebrated lawyer. Wylie himself would seem to qualify as a "real" person since only two or three minor statements about his past life are not demonstrably true.

The first section of *Opus 21*, "Scherzo," opens in August in New York City on a Thursday when Wylie's doctor, Tom Alden, diagnoses a growth in his throat as probably terminal cancer. Wylie decides not to inform Ricky until Monday, when the biopsy report will be available; he returns to his hotel and the labor of cutting forty pages from a recently completed serial. At lunch, he makes the acquaintance of Yvonne Prentiss, a beautiful young married woman from Los Angeles who has left her husband because she had discovered him in a homosexual act. After airing his views on the Kinsey report, Wylie proposes that they continue their discussion at dinner. Alone, again in his room, he reviews his previous encounters with "George T. Death," fights down his fear, and forces himself to his work table. He is interrupted by his nephew, Paul Wilson, a nuclear physicist, with whom he debates his thesis that scientists of the world of objects need to study the subjective realities within themselves. Paul illustrates Wylie's view when he confesses that he is under great stress because he is in love with Marcia, a beautiful whore, who has given up her career to live with him and whom he wants to marry. Wylie agrees to meet her at lunch on Friday. Alone, he meditates on his decision to commit suicide with an overdose of morphine when the pain gets bad. A call from Ricky causes him to recall her ten-year struggle with the results of undulant fever, a series of illnesses which now seems to be over.

"Tarantella" opens with Wylie again encountering Yvonne, who has moved to the room next to his. At dinner he explains his theory of the role of counterpoised instincts and his views on the unnaturalness of sexual taboos. He also discovers that she has an unadmitted fascination with Lesbianism and the compulsion to dominate males; he resists the latter by refusing to humor her moods and, ultimately, disregarding a seduction attempt. Afterward, he pays a call on Hattie Blaine, the madam of a high-priced brothel, in order to learn about Marcia's character. Inevitably, a discussion ensues, with Hattie providing expert testimony on the inadequacies of American wives as sexual partners. Ever keeping an eye open for business, she sends in Gwen Taylor, whose advances Wylie politely discourages. He ends the long evening reading in bed a book on the danger of the population explosion.

"Andante" begins on Friday morning with Wylie at work. His lunch with Paul and Marcia is a social disaster since both Philip and she realize that he once saw her "working" in Miami. He also senses that she is acting a role, pretending to be the girl whom Paul, the adolescent romantic, wants her to be and that she is a true wanton, moved to lust by any male. After an afternoon of work and while on an errand, the narrator observes some members of a veteran's convention "goosing" passing girls with an electrical device; he hits one in the mouth and barely escapes from his buddies. Later, he meets his doctor, Tom Alden, for dinner; they discuss human cruelty, the vicious, wasteful clinging to life of the aged, and Wylie's ideal world, that is based on the Golden Rule of Instinct—to "do unto the unborn generations as they would wish their ancestors had done unto them."

Back at his hotel, Philip is propositioned once again—over the phone—by Gwen Taylor and accepts, mostly out of loneliness. At this point, in the most famous passage in *Opus 21*, he devotes twelve pages to a serio-comic examination of some of the 1,506 reasons, supposedly listed by Forbisher-Laroche, for associating with prostitutes. He soon regrets his impulse to see Gwen and is relieved when Yvonne "borrows" his date after eavesdropping on her talk about her Lesbian encounters. Wylie falls asleep and dreams one of his "fables," one in which civilization collapses when some unknown agency persists in shaping the clouds over the major cities into obscene words which no human effort can erase. At four-fifteen on Saturday morning, he is awakened by Paul, who is nearly deranged by the fact that Marcia has deserted him, allegedly because Philip had disapproved of her.

In "Rondo," leaving his nephew in a drugged sleep, Wylie consults with his friend and lawyer, David Berne, to get advice about Paul and to make his own will. At lunch he again encounters Yvonne, who happily reports that her recent Lesbian experience has liberated her from her life-long inner tensions. Paul departs to look for Marcia, but Wylie's work is interrupted by the liberal churchman, "Socker" Melton, who elicits a complete statement of Wylie's theory of the relationship of religion to the instincts. Later, Wylie, in his bathtub, and Yvonne, in the outer room, discuss homosexuality. When Paul returns at dinner time, Yvonne persuades him to accompany her to night spots to show Marcia that he no longer cares for her. Wylie works until after midnight, when Yvonne returns to report that Paul abandoned her to look for Marcia. Again, she urges Phil to sleep with her. Instead, he goes to Hattie Blaine's to persuade Marcia to tell Paul the truth about herself and thus eventually help him to understand himself; she agrees—on the condition that Philip go to bed with her. He refuses.

Later, Philip dreams a second fable, this one about how Christ materialized on the *Enola Gay* on her way to Hiroshima but failed to persuade the Catholic commander or the atheistic scientist to accept the meaning of His message of love. On Sunday morning, Yvonne returns to her husband, supposedly with new insight into herself and him. When Paul arrives at around four, Philip decides to cure him with the truth; but Paul, incapable of accepting reality, places himself on the parapet outside the window. After Dave Berne saves Paul, who is taken to a psychiatrist, Wylie experiences a severe letdown, spends the evening indulging in self-pity, and falls asleep in his chair feeling very old.

In "Coda," Monday finally comes. He finishes editing the serial and goes to hear his death warrant. To his astonishment and relief, the growth is nonmalignant after all. But then Ricky suddenly arrives—announcing that the undulant fever has returned and that she must face more pain and medical torture. The morning mail reveals that Internal Revenue has decided to examine all of Philip's tax records of 1945 and 1946—all to be assembled immediately at great cost to Wylie in time and money. Then Harold Ober, his literary agent, calls with the news that the editor has decided that he does not want the serial after all—and so a whole summer's work is wasted and the money he had counted on is gone. Wylie, last seen at lunch, is speculating on whether man will learn enough in time to avoid the penalty for willful ignorance of himself—universal madness and death at his own hands in atomic war.

After completing *Opus 21*, the reader has a sense of having shared in an experience, not read about it, and he may explain his reaction by saying that it seemed real because this is a novel without a plot—a slice taken out of life. This explanation, however, is not supported by the facts: *Opus 21* only gives the *impression* of life and is actually a skillfully contrived story—certainly Wylie's most completely successful piece of plot handling and a good illustration of the old theory that the best art is that which conceals itself. In analyzing the plot, we must keep firmly in mind the fact that, except for the basic situation, Wylie invented everything that happened and therefore had a reason for selecting each event that he included. Quite obviously he has chosen as interruptions of the narrator's work schedule only those which will carry out his primary objective—to write a novel in which he can present Jungian ideas. We should also observe that the author manages eventually to cover in the conversations all of the major elements of his philosophy—and that he does so without repetition, an achievement that is surely no easy task or mere accident, but the result of conscious planning.

Perhaps the single most effective element in *Opus 21* is the character portrayal. A possible explanation lies in Wylie's emotional state while composing *Opus 21;* because of his recent traumatic brush with death, he was more than usually aware of the workings of his own inner being and, consequently, that of the characters he was producing from his own mind. As he himself had noted in *Night Unto Night,* men about to die grow very thoughtful. His success with characterizing the three main women may be attributed to the fact that, as an admirer of women, he had observed their actions and talk very carefully and that, as a critic of them, he had developed insight into their complex and often unconscious motivations.

Yvonne Prentiss—the most fully realized of the women

characters—was primarily intended to be an illustration of what was wrong with many American wives. When the narrator meets her, she is well on her way to becoming just one more Common Woman because, basically, she wants to control every man she meets. She has tried to force her husband to become a successful businessman like her father—instead of the botanist he wants to be—by using the withholding of her sexual favors as a weapon. Resentful of Wylie's remarks about the flaws of women, she attempts to seduce him and thereby assert her superiority to him. She regards marriage as a means of acquiring material possessions, not as a union based on love and a mutual giving, and she uses every imaginable device to avoid pregnancy and escape her natural role in life.

Even worse, Yvonne is possessed of nearly invincible ignorance: she has read *Vipers* but sees in it not her own flaws but only the outrageous lies of a man embittered by a woman who rejected him. She regards her husband's single homosexual encounter as proof of his depravity, not understanding that her coldness had pushed him into the relationship or that she, herself, has Lesbian tendencies. Nevertheless, Yvonne has real potential for becoming a good woman because she has some intelligence and eventually is able to understand and even apply Wylie's ideas to her own situation.

Of course, the reader owes much of his knowledge of Yvonne to the narrator's perceptive editorial comments and to her actions, but she becomes a living woman mostly because of Wylie's unfailing accuracy in capturing the sound and inflections of her voice in her changing moods. Indeed, the reader is soon able to tell exactly what she is actually thinking and feeling merely by listening to subtle changes in the sound of her voice. Like the author, the reader soon grows to like Yvonne very much, especially when her good qualities emerge as a result of Wylie's refusal to succumb to either her wiles or her tantrums. Yet Wylie never makes the error of assuming that her experiment with Lesbianism has worked a permanent cure or that she can successfully apply her new knowledge to her real-life relationship with her husband. The reader hopes for the best, but, when she walks out of *Opus 21*, she still emanates that capacity for destructiveness with which she entered it.

Paul Wilson, the victim of Marcia and his own unrealistic views of love and women, is one of Wylie's most disturbing portraits. Although Paul originally was intended by Wylie to serve as an illustration of how a scientist with a disciplined intellect, but with no knowledge of his subjective nature, can be destroyed by his ignorance, the young physicist becomes both a real person and a more universal type—the human being who finds in love only anguish. Paul's personality emerges mostly through dialogue. Our first impression of him, however, comes from the narrator's favorable evaluation of his nephew's achievement as a nuclear scientist, his mental acuity, and his moral earnestness. Despite Paul's amusement at his uncle's views of scientists, he, too, is deeply troubled about the morality of helping to build even more destructive atomic weapons for the government: he is beginning to see that he must live as a man as well as a researcher.

But it is, indeed, as a man that Paul is most ill-prepared for life; he has never learned to accept with grace the things he cannot change or to understand and cope with his feelings about women. Because he had had little money during his student years, he had missed the practical experience with girls that most males receive during adolescence. But more important had been his one-sided education, for nowhere in the curriculum had there been a study of psychology or even a hint that man's subjective reality merited investigation. If anything, Paul's training had taught him to deride psychology, as we can see from his superior attitude toward *Vipers*, which he had read without understanding. Thus, we are treated to an edifying spectacle: a man who has trained himself to be totally objective about the data he observes in his laboratory and to act on the basis of that evidence, but refuses to apply the same methodology to his relationship with Marcia. We feel, nevertheless, that Paul is a kind, likeable, and well-meaning person—hardly deserving of his fate—and, of course, we find a particular appeal in the fact that his idealized view of life and love is infinitely more attractive than the ugly one which we have learned to accept, but never cease to resent.

The best piece of character portrayal in *Opus 21* and, indeed, in all of his works is that of the narrator, Philip Wylie, who, for the purposes of this discussion, is to be treated as a fictional person, just as the author recommended, even though he owes much of his nature to his creator. By this time in his life, the author had attained a degree of acceptance of his own nature and, because he understood the origins of it, could no longer see any point in passing judgments as to what was good or bad in it. Therefore, he was able to set his own character before the reader with something at least approaching the honesty of an impartial observer.

One danger which Wylie, the author, carefully avoided was the temptation to begin speculating on what Philip's *real* nature is—to start one of those apparently endless examinations of motives in a search for the ultimate "true" reason for an action or attitude. Perhaps he had already grown frustrated by this process during psychoanalysis—or perhaps he had come to believe that the nature of a personality is discernible not in its speculation about itself but in its actions. In any case, the reader learns to know Philip Wylie by observing him in action (mental and physical) during a four-day period, which is time enough (considering the stress-filled situation) for both the contradictions and the consistencies to emerge into such meaningful patterns that we may truly say that whoever touches this book touches a man.

Wylie's intention to make *Opus 21* a showcase for his ideas is as successful as his plan to picture himself in the novel. He covers all the matters previously discussed in *Vipers* and in *An Essay on Morals*, adds his newest theories, and presents them all with complete lucidity and with an engaging liveliness that *An Essay* does not have. Moreover, his latest opinions are as intrinsically provocative as his familiar ones and cover an equally wide range of topics. For example, the income-tax system penalizes the creative artist while giving every advantage to makers of bricks and pies. The new fad of air conditioning shows Americans' inability to live naturally in their environment. The Kinsey report on the sex habits of American males has proved what Wylie had been saying for years, but it has been believed only because Americans unquestioningly accept the findings of anyone claiming to be a scientist.

The public's fear of homosexuality is an attempt to conceal their own secret inclinations or past, deliberately forgotten acts. Sex manuals, if written by doctors, can now be sent in the mail, but their mechanistic approach to the sex act puts a premium not on fun or pleasure but on the technique. Man (encouraged by religions that oppose birth control) is overpopulating the planet and consuming irreplaceable resources to satisfy an insatiable desire for things; geriatrics is worsening the situation and should be replaced by voluntary euthanasia. The scientists, by not fighting the military's obsession with secrecy, have allowed them to destroy freedom at home; meanwhile, the Russians are getting ready to attack with their A-bombs—or the improved weapons based on fusion.

The list of negative thoughts goes on and on. But always there is an undertone of hard-core optimism. The dream persists of a world where the people "do unto others as they'd be done by" and "unto the unborn generations as they would wish their ancestors had done unto them." Love—mature, compassionate, fulfilling—does exist—between men and women, between people, regardless of sex. Beauty—in nature, flowers, the sea—can be found, embraced, enjoyed. Blows can be struck—with fists or laughter or acts of selfless giving—against cruelty, ignorance, and shame. Death can be defied with courage; and living, though we are denied even our most modest expectations, is, in the end, enough.

III *A Fable for the Sexes*

Wylie's next book, *The Disappearance* (January, 1951), became, because of its highly original subject, one of his most widely read works; the paperback edition reached its sixth printing as late as 1966. Described by various critics as fantasy, science fiction, doomsday novel, parable, or allegory, the story is actually, to use Wylie's term, a "fable," a sibling of *Gladiator, The Murderer Invisible,* and the short tales in *Finnley Wren* and *Opus 21*—for, like them, *The Disappearance* uses a completely impossible premise or situation to draw attention to its thesis.

In 1950, Wylie turned to the use of the fable again, this time to convey his response to the feminists who, not comprehending his statements about women in *Vipers* and *Opus 21*, were attacking him as a male chauvinist.[1] He decided that the best way of showing what his beliefs really were—that the two sexes should not compete with each other but do their best to fulfill the divergent, equally important, and complementary sexual roles assigned them by nature—was to demonstrate the consequences if one of them completely and suddenly vanished. Later, he decided to include an account of a nuclear war with Russia to demonstrate another important thesis—that such an event, which he believed was inevitable, would cause incredible destruction because of the lack of both military and civilian preparedness.

The Disappearance is set mostly in Miami, Florida, and the story begins in 1950 on Valentine's Day at 4:04 P.M. At that instant all the female human beings disappear from the world which men inhabit, while, simultaneously, in a parallel existence, all the men vanish from the women's world. The novel covers, in alternating sections, the events of the next four years. It centers on the activities of the two main characters, William Percival Gaunt, the philosopher, who, because of his wide knowledge, is renowned as a "generalist," and his wife, Paula, once a brilliant linguist but now living somewhat unhappily the role of wife and mother.

The men, out of habit, continue their usual occupations. However, there is a lot of rioting, looting, panic, and hysteria, and the President declares nationwide martial law. There is also an immediate and real grief and an anguished sense of loss. The Russians, who had been planning an attack anyway, blame the disappearance of their women on the Americans and order the United States to surrender or be destroyed by a nuclear attack. The President refuses; in the short war that ensues, three major cities are hit; but Russia is defeated, surrenders, and forms a non-Communist government.

In the months that follow, a steady deterioration ensues: homosexuality increases, along with female impersonation and all sorts of lewd entertainment, despite the efforts of churchmen to impose "moral" codes; fist fights, riots, and even insurrections break out sporadically in the short-tempered, sexually frustrated populace; the supplying of consumer goods and the operation of public utilities become unreliable; medical treatment is difficult to obtain because there are no nurses. In the meantime, the efforts of the nation's leading scientists to recover the women or to find a means of propagating the race fail completely—and even these great men degenerate into loneliness, despair, alcoholism, and suicide. Then all order collapses, and the men abandon the cities, form into groups of brigands, and begin looting and roaming the country at will. Order is slowly being restored when the four-year ordeal suddenly ends—exactly at the moment when it began, but with everyone's memory intact.

The world of women without men suffers, if possible, an even more horrible fate than that of the men. It becomes evident immediately that women have been mostly the consumers in the civilized nations and that they have had no part in the work that keeps the system functioning and that they do not even know how anything is done. In a few instances, women like Paula Gaunt and her daughter, Edwinna, working with groups of university-trained girls and their teachers, or even with women's club officers, manage to restore some order and operate a few machines. But it becomes clear eventually that those who are trained in technology are too small in number and that replacements for men cannot be trained in time. The heavy industries cannot be revived; the transportation system is inoperative; the supplies of gasoline, cigarettes, canned food, indeed, all manufactured goods, are quickly looted, hoarded, and consumed.

In their attempts at governing themselves and in co-ordinating their efforts, the women are ludicrous, at least at first, when all-female assemblies waste their time in choosing official costumes. When a Russian fleet arrives at New York to demand America's surrender, they do avoid an atomic war, but mostly because Paula, serving as interpreter for Madame President, calls their bluff. Moreover, the American women quickly corrupt their Russian counterparts by exposing them to the luxury items which Stalin had denied them. Nevertheless, after four years, the population has been drastically decimated by natural disasters and epidemics and is reduced to subsistence farming.

In the final chapters, the sexes are miraculously restored to each other. The joy is overwhelming, for the dead are alive and well, the loved ones are united, the loneliness and frustration are gone. Everywhere, people are making love in an incredible orgy, but, as Gaunt notes, "It's the only happy orgy humanity ever had." The happiness seems likely to continue because both men and women now understand the errors in their thinking and behavior that, even before the disappearance, had caused the sexes, in a very real sense, to live in two different and separate worlds.

Men had begun the sexual cold war by treating women merely as erotic toys to be used for sexual pleasure; by so doing, they had denied them their dignity as human beings and had labeled as inferior their awesome role as the mothers of the species. Women had retaliated in predictable ways: with sexual frigidity that made them and their mates into unsatisfied and miserable haters of life; with an insatiable craving for material goods to fill their emotional emptiness; with selfish exploitation and domination of men to obtain those possessions; and with attempts to assume the male role because it seemed to promise self-respect. In the end, both sexes had achieved only self-defeat and loneliness.

Now the human race has a chance to start all over. By comprehending that the roles of the sexes are unequal in function but equal in importance to the prime goal of life—the procreation and proper upbringing of the next generation—men and women will be able to undertake that shared effort with the mutual respect which alone makes possible the giving and receiving of love—the ingredient without which life is barren indeed.

The Disappearance is extraordinarily engrossing reading, not because of any suspense generated by the plot (although we do wonder what perils will come next and whether the sexes will be reunited), but because of the intrinsic interest of each of the parts. Wylie's inventiveness rarely falters, for no subject ever inspired his imagination as much as the horrors attendant upon the massive destruction of man and modern civilization. Consequently, his pictures of the disasters that take place in the parallel monosexual worlds rank with the best in any of his doomsday novels and even with his greatest achievements anywhere. As usual in his works of fantasy, these events owe their ability to compel belief to the documentary-like detail of their setting, which, in this case, is once again Miami, Florida, complete with real street names and every necessary geographic aspect.

A less spectacular but more meaningful accomplishment is Wylie's evocation of the particular kind of loneliness that affects people separated from the opposite sex. He, of course, drew some of his insights on the subject from his own experiences before he married Ricky; but actually he needed only to copy down what he had observed all around him, for the prime affliction of contemporary life is that terrible loneliness that even sexual intimacy cannot dispel because men and women refuse to accept each other as worthy to be loved.

IV   Tomorrow!

Tomorrow! was published in January, 1954, had a hard cover run of three printings, reappeared in a paperback edition in 1963, and sold nearly thirty thousand copies. Perhaps no other Wylie work except *Generation of Vipers* created so much immediate shock as this one, and, though it is today not rated among his better works, no one who has ever read it will be able to erase certain scenes from his mind.

The period during which Wylie served as a consultant to the Federal Civil Defense Administration (1949 to 1954) was a time of unparalleled frustration and anxiety for him because of the failure of America's government and populace to take the actions required to prevent an atomic bomb attack by Russia and to cope realistically with its consequences if it came. Wylie was, from the beginning, certain that the Russians could build nuclear weapons because the "secret" had been common knowledge among physicists since the early 1930s; he was also convinced that the Communist leaders would use the bombs to further their conquest of the world. He knew, too, from his visits to the testing sites in Nevada, that the destructive power of atomic weapons required a whole new approach to civil defense; and, after studying the effect of World War II air raids on civilian populations, he concluded that an unprepared American citizenry would not be able to deal psychologically with a nuclear holocaust.

As a result of Wylie's views and experiences, he decided to outline for the Federal Civil Defense Administration some very practical plans. He advocated the building of an effective early-warning system; the construction of large numbers of air-raid shelters; the organizing and training of firemen, police, and doctors in the proper response to a catastrophe; contingency plans in which unhit cities would aid their less fortunate neighbors; and thorough indoctrination of the populace in order to prepare them mentally. Hardly anything was ever done to carry out these or any other proposals—largely because the public was constantly being misled by its ignorant or foolish political leaders, by a Congress intent on balancing the budget, and by its own tendency toward wishful thinking.

When Wylie could stand the situation no longer, he decided to educate the public by himself.[2] He began publishing articles containing his views, but his first attempt to dramatize them, in 1952, was a scenario for a movie. After it was rejected as too expensive to make—and possibly because the producers knew that no one would voluntarily go to see it, Wylie then in 1953 turned his script into a novel, with which he hoped, as he had in 1941 with *The Other Horseman*, to reach a wide audience.

Wylie set the story in the Midwest, the bastion of isolationism, and he invented two cities separated by a river and a state boundary. Green Prairie has an active Civil Defense program; River City has none. In the first half of the novel, heated debates between the opponents and proponents of preparedness include all of the current shades of opinion. Into the second half of the narrative, which tells of the Russian attack, Wylie put all he knew about the effects of an exploding nuclear weapon. He felt that it was particularly important to stress the nature of the wounds which people can receive in such an attack because most Americans, except for doctors and nurses, had never seen even a single mangled body. Since even the war-toughened Japanese had been overwhelmed by the sight of thousands of people bloodied by flying glass or by "the nearly unendurable" appearance and smell of bad burns, Wylie made a particular effort to fill that vacuum in American education.

The final pages of the novel tell how America replies to the Russian demand for surrender—with a counterattack by an atomic submarine converted into a gigantic hydrogen bomb with a cobalt casing. When the weapon is detonated in the Gulf of Finland, it exterminates most of the enemy population with its explosion and the deadly cloud which it generates. Free at last of the Communist menace, the survivors in America begin to build a new and better world. Wylie had written the ninety-thousand-word novel at his usual high speed; the justly famous five-thousand-word editorial on Civil Defense dictated by Coley Borden in the story took Wylie only two hours—the explanation, as he later reported, was that he knew exactly what he wanted to say, having thought about it for a long time.[3]

In a propaganda novel one often finds very little effort at characterization—but *Tomorrow!* is certainly an exception. As each person is introduced, Wylie discusses him at some length, sometimes devoting several pages to an essay on his social origins, to experiences that either molded his character or revealed it, and even to rather explicit listings of traits. He probably realized that *Tomorrow!* would lose much of its impact if the people in it did not seem like recognizable fellow human beings to the reader. Most of the portraits, however, suffer from too much reliance on direct authorial comment and too little use of their thoughts. Furthermore, Wylie tends to stereotype his cast, making the good people (the advocates of Civil Defense) paragons of virtue in their every action and the bad ones (the apathy delegation) guilty of everything from racial prejudice to embezzlement.

There are two notable exceptions. Nora Conner, for instance, is the best picture he ever drew of a pre-adolescent because he focuses on her thoughts and feelings. Similarly, the editor, Coley Borden, makes a lasting impression on us—again because we have access to his personal world. Wylie tells us in the beginning that Coley had in his lifetime loved four people very deeply—and that all of them had been taken from him in ways that were all different but all extremely painful. Though Coley is only fifty-two (Wylie's age), his life force is nearly gone, used up in his past struggles to endure the unbearable. He has a longing for peace that is stronger than his instinct for survival or his sympathies for others. He is not in despair—he is merely detached. He is thus able to watch the approaching guided missile, observe its details, calculate its objective, foresee its effect—up to the very instant when the light "burst down toward him."

There is no doubt that this picture of Coley is a self-portrait, for at this time Wylie, too, was often melancholy and given to grim meditations about how many of his own family had died in meaningless ways and about how his efforts to bring reforms had always failed. Often he must have wished, like Coley, to see the end of the world of foolishness and suffering—and to hear the great silence afterward. Moods like these, which his regular consultations with a psychoanalyst did little to cure, were a grim forewarning of the emotional collapse which lay just ahead of him.

One really surprising aspect of *Tomorrow!* is that Wylie includes a number of ideas besides his primary one about the need for civil defense. Indeed, in the opening pages, we get the impression that the book is to be a novel of manners about life in a Midwestern city or perhaps a satire on the hypocrisy and the materialism of suburbia. Further on, we find a section on the quality of television programs and their audiences that is as vicious and funny as the comments on radio in *Vipers*. Wylie also attacks the ugliness of slums and the strangulation of cities by the automobile, and he protests against the destruction of natural beauty and animal life by pollution and urban sprawl. Another of his favorite targets—the irresponsible newspaper—is condemned by Wylie's fictional example of a slanted news story, one which begins with the wholly inaccurate headline, "Sixteen Hurt in CD Alert."

Also found in *Tomorrow!* are a number of Wylie's most deeply held feelings. As in *The Disappearance*, he argues that the Russians must be dealt with by a massive display of power, and he has no patience with those who argue that the United States must not jeopardize the chances for peace proposals by any actions or statements that will make the Reds antagonized or suspicious. In *Tomorrow!*, Wylie also continues his attack on prejudice against Jews and Negroes.

On the subject of sex, Wylie is consistent with his earlier views: sexual behavior or "misbehavior" is normal because human beings are animals with strong sex drives; "shocked" disapproval, on the other hand, is despicable hypocrisy or the result of elaborate self-deceit. By contrast, the author has only scorn for those of the "well-born and well-heeled classes" who explain "loose sex manners in a mother" as "feminist pioneering" or as "what the country club set does for fun."

Still, Wylie's main purpose was to warn the public of the price of being unprepared for nuclear war, and his descriptions of the victims of an A-bomb attack are indescribably horrible, drawn from the hellish nightmares of a man obsessed with the extremities of human suffering. One example is sufficient: "He said something like, owowowowowowowowowo, and began to run down the sidewalk. . . . Between the sounds he emitted, the man *clicked* as he ran . . . . Both the man's feet were gone and he was running on the ends of his shinbones." Such passages in *Tomorrow!* caused a tremor of shuddering—as well as cries of outrage at Wylie's bad taste—mostly from the very people he was trying to educate about the realities of atomic war.

As it turned out, *Tomorrow!* never had a real chance to change public sentiment or governmental policy, for, later on in 1954, the Russians detonated an operational model of a hydrogen bomb. Thus, in an instant, all of the programs for civil defense became irrelevant—because nothing could survive an H-bomb blast. But, ironically, for Wylie one nightmare was over: he declared at once that there was no longer any danger of nuclear war because now no one had any chance of surviving.[4]

V   The Oracle of the Atomic Age

On May 7, 1955, *The Answer*, a short novelette by Wylie (about fifteen thousand words), appeared in the *Saturday Evening Post*. It was accompanied by laudatory comments by Bernard Baruch, Milton Eisenhower, Eleanor Roosevelt, Norman Vincent Peale, and Carl Sandburg. Having received widespread acclaim, this narrative ran through at least four printings in hard covers in April of the next year, and it was printed in paperback form in 1963.

Wylie was himself very fond of *The Answer* because in writing it he had been able to do easily something the "experts" had claimed couldn't be done. The idea, he told me in 1970, occurred to him in 1954 in Colorado: "Wouldn't it be funny if one of the bomb tests brought an angel down?" When he mentioned the premise to "several writers who were teachers, they looked a little askance as people do when they hear an idea like *The Disappearance*." After returning home to Rushford, New York, Wylie composed the whole story in only two days, and he worked out the details of the plot with all the self-confidence of one who had done this kind of thing many times before. The only major addition to his original plan was to have the Russians down a second angel. The characters were purely fictional, with one exception: the Russian premier was modeled on Malenkov, Stalin's successor, "the prune-eyed fat guy" whom Wylie detested.

The Answer begins in the spring of a year in the relatively near future as Major General Marcus Scott observes the explosion of the latest American H-bomb at a Pacific test site. Later, he is called to a nearby island to examine the only casualty: a beautiful human-like creature that looks like an angel. The witness to its death is a minister's nine-year-old son, who reports that its last words were "I was a little too late." Reverend Simms goes completely berserk and tries to kill the soldiers who are removing the body of "Gabriel." Scott establishes tight security at once; the President is informed; and the body is placed on a plane bound for Washington. When the aircraft is lost en route, the President must suppress all information about the incident in order to prevent panic; because he does not know the angel's mission, all he can do is wait to see whether retaliation, divine or extraterrestial, will come.

In the middle of the summer, the Russians, testing their own bomb, knock down another angel, who is shot to death by the guards, along with the trespassing peasant who had found him. The Russian Premier flies to the scene; he orders an autopsy and destruction of the remains by attaching it to the next day's test bomb. His motive is that a revival of religion would overthrow him and the Communist plans for world domination.

When General Scott returns to the United States testing ground at Christmas, he persuades the minister's son to reveal the whole story of the angel's last moments. He learns that the being had brought a golden book containing "Wisdom gathered from our whole galaxy—for earth" and written in every language. The boy, like the Russian peasant, had concealed it with the hope of selling it because he was poor. In the book, Scott reads the answer to the world's dilemma: "Love one another."

The Answer was written to dramatize one of the central ideas from *An Essay on Morals*—the effect of dogma on the minds of those who have committed themselves to the defense of every detail of their faith rather than to the never-ending search for truth. When faced with new information, these persons, whether Christians or

Communists, feel personally threatened; and they do so with good reason, for to accept such data is to admit that their actions and their goals in life have been built on falsehoods. Unlike more humble men trained to accept the possibility of error, they can no longer think or act rationally: instead, they destroy the evidence, exterminate or neutralize those who think differently, and pretend to themselves that nothing ever happened. The angels in *The Answer* are, in effect, *reality;* and the most important message in the story is not that man can find salvation through loving his fellows; rather the point is that salvation can come only through loving truth, a far more difficult enterprise.

This little novel has two flaws. One is that the loss of the first angel by an accident, though possible in life, seems improbable in fiction. The second is that the story is cast in the form of a parable, a simple narrative without any inserted explanation of what the events mean; therefore, some readers will certainly miss the point, especially if they are not familiar with Wylie's ideas. In fact, many misunderstood even the import of the message carried by the angels. Judging by the response of Norman Vincent Peale, many readers assumed that "the answer" in Wylie's book would save the world. They overlooked two facts: that the messengers had not provided salvation—but only a tool with which men could save themselves—and that the message was the same one which Jesus of Nazareth had given mankind—with no appreciable results—nearly two thousand years ago. Philip Wylie's irony had escaped them.

CHAPTER 8

Years of Decline

WYLIE'S output from 1957 to 1967 was marked by a serious decline in quality as well as in quantity, both of which caused a long downward slide of his literary reputation. The causes were many. One was the demise of the magazines which had provided him with a regular income for nearly thirty years; *American, Saturday Evening Post, Collier's, Cosmopolitan,* and *Redbook* either ceased publication or tried new formats as television stole their readers. At the same time, more and more of his pieces were rejected by editors because they were looking for newer, fresher material; and Wylie no longer could grasp what they and their audiences wanted. There was money to be made in writing for the new medium, but Wylie did not want to give up the advantages of his life as a free-lancer to become a salaried member of the writing teams that bore an unpleasant resemblance to those he had worked on in Hollywood in the 1930s.

Unfortunately, other schemes for making money had also evaporated. The Crunch and Des television series died, two scripts for movies set in Florida came to nothing when the companies changed their minds, and a book started in 1948 was abandoned after eight years. Wylie's situation worsened as the 1960s began. As we shall see, his book on the Slater Enterprises earned him nothing when he and a former friend parted company. He then began work on *Images of God* in August, 1960; by the next April, it was in trouble. It was summarily rejected by a new editor at the recently reorganized Holt, Rinehart, and Winston in November, rewritten, and again turned down. In a rage, Wylie severed his ties with the company after thirty-one years; and they, accusing him of contract violations, sold the paperback rights to all his older books to recover their losses.

In 1966 he was at work on a philosophical work on ecology, "Unto the Third Generation"; its unfinished manuscript is still among his papers, as is a long work about his boyhood, called "Boy Into Man." Except for *Triumph*, his published books sold poorly. Meanwhile, the losses accumulated: in November, 1963, a fire at his Rushford, New York, home nearly cost him his life and caused repair bills that far exceeded the amount of insurance coverage. The next year he had to sell the Florida home he had built for Ricky. Perhaps the low point in his fortunes was reached in 1967, when at age sixty-five he tried to collect on his endowment insurance policy and discovered that his borrowings on it over the years had rendered it worthless.

Aside from bad luck and the changing requirements of his potential audience, the problem was in Wylie himself. The physical and mental strain of twenty-five years at the typewriter had shown up suddenly when he reached fifty: overnight, according to some of his friends, he aged in appearance. His anxiety over the dangers of the atomic age and his frustration over the ignorant response of America had also drained him. Then, as the sources of money dried up, he began to worry, and, as he brooded, he lost his confidence; with it went inexorably the energy needed to create the new ideas required for his books and the effective expression of them.

In desperation, trying to cure his acrophobia, nervousness, and depression, he had gone into intense analysis in Baltimore in 1952 and 1953. At that time his doctor began prescribing amphetamines to help him conquer his low spirits. Wylie soon came to rely on them, and on the alcohol that made him violent and impossible to live with. By 1957 he was so badly dependent on it that he swallowed his pride enough to join Alcoholics Anonymous. That experiment lasted until June, 1960, but he was sober only technically because he increased his use of the amphetamines and was, by his own confession, an addict from 1958 to 1966. Inevitably, his marriage suffered, and Ricky, also, often drank too much. For whole months he couldn't find the energy or ability to write; when he did, his drug-induced euphoria completely destroyed his once keen ability to evaluate his work. It is little wonder that so much of his material was rejected, or that those who knew him well were sure that he was finished.

I   The Innocent Ambassadors

In May, 1957, the Rinehart Company published *The Innocent Ambassadors*, a 140,000 word piece of non-fiction. Like *Finnley*

Wren, Generation of Vipers, An Essay on Morals, and *Opus 21,* it has a flamboyantly baroque subtitle: "Being an account of a trip around the world and a compendium of data not found in standard guidebooks . . . . certain candid autobiographical fragments and various biographical notes about the author's wife, a fine woman . . . . a survey of places, both exotic and troubled, undertaken in these terrifying times . . . . along with diverse psychological observations, philosophical comments, horrid sights, vivid insights, assorted enjoyments, revelations, practical suggestions for the salvation of liberty and sundry flights of fancy (not to mention 27,500 miles of literal travel by air) . . . . in sum, a perfectly wonderful book that anybody would be fascinated to read."

Philip and Ricky's trip began on January 31, 1956, lasted nearly three months, and cost him about twenty thousand dollars, an expenditure made possible by one of his most remunerative years. On their way around the globe, they made stops of varying length in Hawaii, Japan, Hong Kong, Thailand, India, Lebanon, Turkey, Greece, Italy, and France. After they returned home, writing *The Innocent Ambassadors* proved to be an ordeal. This author who had once produced a novel in ten days found himself laboring for ten months. He was plagued by worry, indecision, and mental drought, as he admitted to an interviewer from *Life.*[1] Worn out by the trip and a serious illness in Greece, he had returned to work too soon; his stint in the University of Colorado writers' workshop (July 23 to August 12) sapped his remaining energy. Even worse was the emotional exhaustion brought on by the deaths of his father, Ricky's mother, and Robert Lindner, his friend and analyst, all in a brief period of three months.

Understandably, *The Innocent Ambassadors* is not a very good book. In the first place, it does not give the reader very strong impressions of the places which the Wylies visited—certainly a remarkable quality for any travel book, even one intended to be primarily a commentary rather than a travelogue of tourist attractions. Furthermore, its pace is excruciatingly slow. One reason is that long sections are merely lengthy transcriptions of Wylie's conversations with the many people he encountered on his trip. In addition, perhaps as much as three-fourths of *The Innocent Ambassadors* is devoted to extended, inserted essays on the subjects which interested the author. In fact, hardly an incident occurs which does not inspire pages of commentary on philosophy, religion, politics, psychology, human sexual behavior, the Communist threat, or the author's earlier experiences.

Basically, the central thesis of *The Innocent Ambassadors* is that America is well on its way to losing the Cold War with Russia because Americans—and especially their leaders—are almost willfully ignorant of certain vital facts. The chief one is that the Communists, aware that thermonuclear weapons can never be used by either side to conquer the world, have embarked on a campaign to win control of it by means of ideological warfare. Thus, the American efforts to increase their nuclear stockpiles and to form military alliances are pointless, and, even worse, such actions are cited by the enemy as proof that the United States is an imperialist power.

The subject to which Wylie returns nearly as often as foreign policy is religion, but with a significant change in emphasis from that of his earlier books. No longer does he portray himself as the implacable enemy and scorner of all organized religion, clergymen, or believers. Instead, he stresses the idea that all dogmas arise from "a real process" and that the truly religious in all creeds make "themselves neither masters of love, nor its servants, but love's embodiment, thereby . . . revealing the nature of their beliefs by their acts."

There is an ominous quality to such a changed viewpoint, for it does not sound like Wylie at all. The same is true of his mild and forgiving attitude toward human folly and cruelty and especially of his sentimentalizing over love as the salvation of the world. To anyone who knew Wylie personally or through his books, it was clear that something very bad was happening in a troubled mind.

II   Triumph

Nearly six years passed before Wylie was able to produce a publishable work. Finally, in February, 1963, *Triumph*, an account of the destruction of the Northern Hemisphere in a thermonuclear war, was released by his new publisher, Doubleday, giving him a much needed success financially and psychologically. It had been written as a serial for *McCall's* but rejected, apparently because its gory descriptions were unsuitable for a magazine audience. Then Doubleday accepted the 120,000 word narrative, and the *Saturday Evening Post* issued an abridged version from which the most gruesome parts had been removed.

Triumph, set in the early 1970s, opens on the last Thursday in July as Ben Bernman, a young atomic physicist, arrives as a weekend guest at the Connecticut estate of millionaire Vance Farr. Ben is in love with Farr's daughter, Faith, but, unluckily, he is poor, unattractive, and Jewish; furthermore, she is now engaged to Kit Barlow, the playboy and athlete. At 10:30 A.M. on Friday, an all-out thermonuclear attack by planes and rockets is launched against America by Russia. Eventually, fourteen people find safety in Farr's multi-million dollar private bomb shelter located in caverns protected by five hundred feet of rock. This group, along with its complement of WASPS (White Anglo-Saxon Protestants), includes members of various American "minority groups."

By using sophisticated electronic equipment and remote controlled antennae, the survivors are able to follow the progress of the war as the two nations destroy each other over and over. Even China, Russia's supposed ally, is struck, along with Britain and France, by the Russians. Globe-circling clouds of fall-out dump their invisible poisons on the entire North Temperate Zone. After forty-two days, the Russians cautiously emerge from their mountain and ocean floor fortresses—only to be detected by an American missile submarine, which relays its discovery to the scattered units of "Operation Last Ditch"—five submarines and a carrier. Nevertheless, just before the Russians are hit and wiped out, they launch Phase IV of their plan—three hundred bombs with cobalt-jackets—to make North America unliveable for generations because of the long half-life of cobalt. The Russians also annihilate the American naval units.

Meanwhile, back in Farr's redoubt, almost everyone displays racial tolerance, courage, and patience. Kit, however, cannot overcome his claustrophobia, makes his way outside without a shielded suit, and, despite Ben's efforts to save him, dies of the effects of radiation. Faith holds out for two years and two months before she finally admits to Ben that she loves him. After twenty-six months as cave-dwellers, the survivors are lifted by a shielded helicopter to safety on a lead-protected Australian destroyer. They are told of the new world federation being formed in the Southern Hemisphere, where the Anzacs have armed themselves with nuclear weapons and are forcing forever an end to war, racism, and nationalism, as the United States should have done in 1945. But, when the thirteen Americans depart, the United States is no more.

Wylie's account of the thermonuclear war, which occupies only seventeen percent of the book, is an extraordinary performance. His descriptions of the destructive effect of exploding H-bombs may never be surpassed by anyone, and his recital of the physical wounds and psychotic behavior of the victims rivals that in *Tomorrow!* Equally impressive is his inventiveness in devising futuristic military hardware or—to be more accurate—his skill as a prophet, for nearly every one of his nightmares of technology was operational within ten years. It would be wise to read only these parts of *Triumph* and to skip the rest of the pages, which recount impossible feats of technology, improbable acts of heroism, unlikely triumphs of reason over racial prejudice, and, as a change of pace, the boring attempts of the survivors to entertain themselves with reading and roller-skating.

Luckily, Wylie's main theme is clear and overwhelmingly convincing: the awesome power of thermonuclear weapons guarantees that no nation can survive a war in which they are used. Perhaps *Triumph's* message was heard, for, not long afterward, President Kennedy stopped listening to the optimistic prophecies of the Rand Corporation and of military men trained to think in terms of conventional explosives and, instead, pushed forward the negotiations that led to the nuclear test ban. Nevertheless, to this day both Russia and America continue to add to their stockpiles of weapons that they can never use.

III   They Both Were Naked

Wylie's second book for Doubleday, *They Both Were Naked*, was completed on April 1, 1965, and published in October, 1965. Sales were so poor (12,373) that the company lost a great deal of money. Four years later Wylie asserted that it was the worst book he had ever written and that he had deliberately produced a "dirty" story in the vain hope that it would sell a lot of copies and thus help him get out of debt.[2] In this instance, his evaluation of his work's literary merits is almost correct, but his memory is at fault about the level of his aspirations. The novel was, in reality, intended to be a serious sequel to *Opus 21* in its form and content: it is a fictionalized first-person narrative with "Philip Wylie" as a main character, and it contains his current opinions and comments on everything that interested him.

The novel is based on an experience that began one day in 1959 when John Slater (Wylie's boyhood friend in Montclair; the husband of his sister Verona; and a very successful businessman) proposed that he give up free-lancing and write a book about

Slater's career, during which he had founded a nationwide food-services company. Wylie, needing money badly, agreed; he did the interviewing and research on Slater's company and then wrote his book; but, by that time, he had become bitterly disillusioned with Slater, both as a man and as a businessman. Rather than sign his name to a piece of flattering falsehood, he put the manuscript away with other unpublished material. It was a costly decision because he now had to sell his home in Florida in order to pay his debts.

Wylie was, however, able to salvage something from his abortive experience as a biographer, for, when he began work on a new novel, he decided to use it as the basic framework of his story. Two important episodes in it were inspired by other recent real-life events. One was a conversation he had had with two young married couples in which the women spoke openly of how they promoted their husbands' careers by having sexual relations with the head of the company. The other was a scandal involving a boyhood acquaintance who had seduced his daughter-in-law and had thus caused his son's suicide. Most of the novel, however, is pure invention. His main character, Ludie Phyfe, is a composite figure, a kind of archetypal American businessman of the 1960s, and he is not—as Wylie was careful to point out to me—a portrait of John Slater.

Though the main plot concerns the conflict which gradually arises between Ludie and Wylie as the latter becomes aware of his subject's true character, most of the novel consists of secondary plots involving at least nine other people whose lives impinge upon Ludie's and who in various ways contribute to his slide into moral decadence and eventual financial ruin. Wylie, by having such a large cast of characters, was able to dramatize at least a dozen of his favorite themes; but he paid a high price for that privilege—a book without unity or real focus. At least three main plots are occurring simultaneously; and, because he cannot resist the temptation to explore at length the possibilities of each and every subplot, he hopelessly overcrowds the novel with irrelevant material. Adding to the problem are autobiographical fragments, inserted essays, and miscellaneous digressions. Thus, a reader finds himself wandering in a welter of episodes (fifty-seven chapters in all) and often entirely loses sight of the chief characters and, even in retrospect, cannot determine what the novel's main theme is or, indeed, if it has one.

Despite these weaknesses, *They Both Were Naked* might have attained at least a modest success if it had been well written; but it is not. Wylie's diction is pretentious, polysyllabic, and full of newly coined words; and, in a surprisingly high number of instances, he is using words incorrectly or, at least, in a way that is not idiomatic. The really sad aspect of his style is, however, the unbelievably large number of whole sentences (nearly a hundred, in fact) which are either awkwardly phrased, hard to follow, or incomprehensible. In fact, not since *An Essay on Morals* had he been guilty of such unclear writing and never before of so much of it. Obviously he was not thinking very clearly, but some of the obscurity can be attributed to a bad habit that would also plague readers in his future books—his use of his oral style of expression, which hardly makes sense when put on a page.

One of the few outstanding qualities of the novel is the delineation of Ludie Phyfe, which must be considered one of Wylie's most successful creations, even though we can get the full impact of it only by re-reading just those scenes in which Ludie appears. Wylie's achievement is especially impressive because the narrator only gradually becomes aware that the subject of his biography is not the person he seems to be; indeed, he resists, for both personal and financial reasons, facing the implications of the facts he has uncovered. The reader, therefore, has an opportunity to arrive at the truth before Wylie does, particularly by listening to Ludie during his conversations, which seem to reveal a generous, almost naively upright character, but which, when seen in retrospect, cleverly project an image that will favorably impress his audience.

Most of the in-depth insights into Phyfe are given by Wylie himself, who brings his knowledge of psychology to bear on what he recalls of Ludie's personality in his formative years and what he is now learning by observing his actions. Ludie, he sees, owes his success to his ability to discern the weaknesses of others and thereby to control them for his own ends without their knowledge and while giving the impression that he is a well-meaning and highly ethical person. It is appropriate that the two women most responsible for *his* destruction are able to ruin him because they have discovered his weakness—his unacknowledged perverted sexual longings—and exploit it.

We should note, too, that Ludie is not a static character. In the course of the novel, as he succumbs to his inner compulsions and commits the forbidden sins he had secretly dreamed of performing, these acts define and re-shape his character until even his judgment is impaired. He comes to believe that he is all-powerful and then foolishly shows the world his contempt by dropping his facade. This

change in personality is wholly convincing, and it is quite a performance for an author who claimed that he wasn't very adept at
character drawing.

Nearly as good as the portrait of Ludie are those of the major
women characters. They, too, are made to come to life through a
combination of self-revealing speeches and actions and authorial
analysis of their personalities. Both Zenia Taylor, the incestuous
daughter-in-law, and Dianne Fletcher, the wife who sleeps with
Ludie in return for his influence, are chilling case studies of
emasculating American wives who make a career of using men to
achieve their selfish objectives. Their conversations with Wylie are
in themselves revelations of their methods: flattery, cajolery, a tan-
talizing glimpse of the possibility of sexual favors, then nagging,
emotional blackmail, and threats, all concluded by an exit complete
with "butt-twitching triumph." These two women, however, are
carefully individualized by having entirely different personal
backgrounds and, most important, quite dissimilar voices, accents,
and vocabularies.

One of Wylie's major concerns in the novel is to dispel the myths
surrounding the American businessman. For instance, Wylie says,
his "public service" always, in the end, proves to be profitable to his
company. He does not use his leisure and wealth to improve the
quality of his life because he has no other goal in life except to make
money. He claims to have given America a high "standard of
living," but in reality all he has done is to deplete the natural
resources of the continent to make unnecessary products. Worst of
all, he has corrupted the whole populace with a moral code that
justifies any means of acquiring money.

Wylie also uses the novel to present his theories on incest. Recent
scientific findings, he notes, have revealed that human beings, unlike other animals, are responsive from birth to erotic stimulation;
therefore, it is perfectly natural for children to feel sexually attracted to those with whom they have close physical contact, especially their parents. However, because of strong social taboos,
children soon learn to hide these feelings, even from themselves.
These repressed desires, though retaining their original energy in
the unconscious mind, usually affect only one's choice of a mate
and the content of one's sexual fantasies. However, if the forbidden
relationship was once very intense, it can prevent the formation of
normal sexual relationships. Wylie also speculates that the strong
guilt feelings caused in people by the taboo against incest account

for the extreme, almost psychotic, self-righteous attitudes of many persons toward so-called sexual offenders. He therefore concludes by urging biologists and psychologists to study the whole question in order to help mankind to cope with a biological condition unique among animals.

CHAPTER 9

The Last Years (1966-1971)

I N the years remaining to Wylie, he proved beyond any doubt that his greatness as a writer and a man was still there. His five last published works include a superb adventure story, two frighteningly possible predictions of how mankind will come to its end, and a complete statement of his philosophical and ethical beliefs. These accomplishments, which surpass anything he had done since *Opus 21* and *Tomorrow!*, were brought about despite increasingly bad health and a continuation of the same financial and personal problems that had nearly immobilized his creative talents for a decade. Now, however, Wylie was refusing to succumb to discouragement: he fought off his dependence on drugs and alcohol, drove himself to his typewriter, and worked on and on, sometimes finding the old joy that made the words leap from his fingers, usually not, but going on anyway.

The source of Wylie's strength in these years was his involvement in another great crusade—that of the ecologists to save the planet from man himself. It was the most important battle that men had ever undertaken, overshadowing the troubles in Vietnam, in the Middle East, and even in the heart of Philip Wylie, a brave old man who would die without regaining the glory of those days when everyone recognized his name and his only serious worry was whether his shrubbery would survive the visits of tourists.

I *The Philosophy Complete*

When Wylie's third book for Doubleday, *The Magic Animal: Mankind Revisited,* was published on April 5, 1968, it was advertised as a worthy successor to *Generation of Vipers;* actually, its nearest relative is *An Essay on Morals*, for it is a long (one hundred thirty thousand words) and detailed statement of the foundations and implications of the author's philosophy of life. Also, like *An*

Essay on Morals, it is an attempt to explain what the author believes in and is *for* rather than what he is against. And, like its predecessor, it offers a program for saving mankind from a rapidly approaching day of doom. The chief difference is that this time he sees the extinction of man as certain and not merely probable, as it had been in the early days of the Atomic Age.

The Magic Animal, like his earlier philosophical works, was the end product of a long search for a valid explanation of the meaning of existence and for a moral code based on that interpretation. The process had begun when Wylie grew dissatisfied with the conclusions he had reached in *An Essay on Morals;* he had discovered that he could no longer accept Jung's mystical pronouncements and that he could not find in Freud any real basis for a moral system. Years passed, however, before, in three separate books, he came upon the germinal ideas from which grew his ultimate philosophy of life.

The first, Joseph Wood Krutch's *The Great Chain of Life* (1957), placed the death of the individual in the context of evolutionary progress: its demise is the last of the series of sacrifices made by an animal both to maintain its species and to push its kind forward in the endless process of change. Here, Wylie saw, was the fundamental moral directive that guides all living beings: all actions that lead to reproduction and proper upbringing of the next generation are good; all that hinder that goal are bad; all other "moral laws" are irrelevant.

The second book, *On Aggression* (1966), by Konrad Lorenz, probably the greatest living student of animal behavior, demonstrated to Wylie conclusively that learning patterns in animals are heavily governed by instinct. Lorenz thus confirmed what Wylie had known since observing animals in Canada in 1920—that "human" behavior is really common to many mammals; that the "gap" between man and other animals is quantitative, not qualitative; and that many instincts of "lower" creatures will also be found in man. The third influential book was Robert Ardrey's *The Territorial Imperative* (1966), which explained how animals are required by instinct to find and defend certain territories against all rivals and enemies in order to provide the living space necessary for the maintenance of their next generation. This thesis gave Wylie, as we shall see, a good explanation for human resistance to new ideas.

The Magic Animal, which cost him two years of work, is a full statement of Wylie's philosophical position in 1968. He begins with certain fundamental principles which, he says, have been established and proven by the scientific method. In the beginning was matter—and nothing else. Eons later, life appeared—because "life is a property of matter that appears under suitable conditions and evolves while such conditions persist." The coming of life was inevitable, given the conditions on this planet and the vast amounts of time available; and so also was the evolution toward more complex life forms as some gene changes proved to be useful by giving the possessor "a slight superiority in the common effort to survive."

The invention of sexual reproduction, which speeds up the evolutionary process by vastly increasing the numbers of each generation, also brought about the necessity for the death of all members of each generation in its turn, for, without such a limitation on population growth, the world would become so congested that a few species would crowd out all other species and finally die out themselves when they had used up all the food available. They would thus bring about the end of nature's evolutionary process, "since it has involved a production of the greatest possible number of species, not merely the greatest numbers in a few kinds."

In the two million years of man's existence as a species, he was able to survive and eventually dominate over all other species because he evolved the ability to imagine—to create and use images and symbols. By this means, he was able to enter what Wylie calls a new "territory," future time. The advantage was that man could plan ahead and "act in ways no longer limited by instinct," and he became a "magic animal." The liability of such a talent was that he now had foreknowledge of his own demise. Since he could see that all animals died, he devised a remarkable strategem to escape the common fate: he asserted that he was not an animal and therefore not doomed to death. He then invented (thus misusing his "magic" powers) the various gods whose immortal essence he supposedly shared; he worked out systems of pleasing these gods in exchange for an "ecstatic immortality."

Wylie observes that these systems invariably were based on the feeling that some behavior was "good" and some was "bad." This phenomenon is an additional demonstration of animal instincts functioning in man, for all animals have a built-in compulsion to do what is "right" for their kind and to avoid the wrong. Although this compulsion remains in man, he has not understood that the basis of morality is the need to maintain the species and that "right" behavior is that which serves the continuity of the species.

Churches, Communism, and capitalism have merely institutional-
ized his error, and they are bringing man close to extinction as he
pollutes the air and water of the planet which his children will in-
herit.

Wylie turns next to a problem which had perplexed him all of his
life: why do men hold on to their beliefs with such fanaticism that
they refuse to alter them in the face of all evidence and will die for
them or kill others with different notions? Mere egotism and
possessiveness can hardly explain such behavior. In an idea
developed from Ardrey, Wylie says that when man started to
employ his imagination to use time as if it were another dimension,
his error was to forget that the images and symbols in his mind
were, in fact, imaginary and unreal. In other words, man began to
think of his beliefs as being real territory; naturally, at that moment
the full power of man's age-old animal instinct to defend territory
began to function. Not to do so *seems* wrong, and no animal can act
against its innate guidelines of right and wrong. Wylie argues that
now that the existence of this instinct—and especially its effect on
beliefs—is established, mankind can free himself from its effect on
his mind and permit his brain to achieve its true function: to hold
"all present fact and truth as tentative and subject to revision, eter-
nally," for "our brain is designed to find and feed on knowledge."

Next, Wylie turns to some of the aspects of animal behavior
which man, unfortunately, does not share. Other creatures do not,
except by accident, murder each other while defending territory or
competing for mates; they do not intentionally wipe out other life
forms; and they do not violate the prime directive concerning the
continuation of the species. Why is man, Wylie then asks, so evil
when other animals are moral? The answer, he believes, lies in
man's basic error—his unwarranted assumption—made necessary
by his fear of death—that he is not an animal, is both superior to
and different from animals, and is therefore not subject to the laws
of nature. Nothing, however, can stifle man's instinctual inner
knowledge of the truth about himself, and therefore he is driven to
actions by which he hopes to convince himself of his alleged
superiority. His most common demonstration of it is the killing of
all other life forms; the "logic" is simple: if he can kill it, he is
superior to it. He kills his own kind, wipes out his fellow species,
and pillages his environment for his own selfish ends.

These actions, of course, result in an increasingly unbearable
sense of guilt, for man has violated the prime directives of nature,

the knowledge of which he shares with all animals. His punishment will be that which comes to any species which interferes with any of the laws of nature that are designed to assure the forward thrust of evolution—extinction. The ageless law is inescapable: man is an animal; he is dependent upon the environment which produced him; and, having corrupted it, he will die with it.

The Magic Animal does offer the possibility of hope for mankind (provided, of course, that there is still time for his sins against nature to be expunged). What is required, says Wylie, is nothing less than a complete reorientation in human thought: not until all men give up their beliefs in gods and in personal immortality will they dedicate their lives to the welfare of those who will follow them; not until then will they realize that man's only immortality is that part of him which survives in his descendants.

A world government is a prerequisite because these changes must be planet-wide. The population must be cut back drastically, and all future breeding must be regulated by geneticists, first, to eliminate the chance of faulty persons being born, and, second, to improve the race by selective mating. The city must be abandoned or drastically altered so as to provide living space. Industrialization for the sake of producing "consumer goods" must be eliminated. All new scientific discoveries, especially those in pharmacology, must be carefully tested before being unleashed on the planet. Meanwhile, social scientists will have the task of devising a sexual morality based upon the realities of man's unique ability to experience sexual pleasure from infancy to senility.

II *The Last Great Adventure Story*

In November, 1969, Doubleday released a new novel by Wylie, *The Spy Who Spoke Porpoise*, which recounts the exploits of Ring Grove, an Office of Strategic Services operative in World War II and now a millionaire toy manufacturer, as he finds himself involved in counter-espionage in contemporary Hawaii. In these adventures, he is working as a special agent for the President, and his enemies include not only Russian and Chinese spies, but the Federal Bureau of Investigation and Central Intelligence Agency as well. Ultimately, after many close scrapes with death, Grove uncovers a Communist plot to destroy Oahu, dispatches his enemies, and proves to himself that a man thinking can be a match for all the technological gadgetry and all the psychological weapons that modern espionage can muster.

Apparently no one at Doubleday had much regard for the novel, for there was no effort to promote it. The book is not even mentioned in the company's extensive pre-Christmas advertisements, and the fact that there were only four reviews of it (a total of perhaps four hundred words) suggests that no copies were sent to the critics. Nevertheless, it sold fairly well on its own, but only for a short time (12,942 in all). The now familiar pattern was repeated: another flop. The only difference in this case is that the book is certainly his best since *Tomorrow!* and is also probably the most completely entertaining novel he ever wrote—the work of a professional at the height of his powers. It is difficult to think of any other story by Wylie with a more suspense-filled plot, more bone-chilling episodes, or more effortless descriptions of both settings and physical action. Most important, this novel also contains one of his most unforgettable heroes and Wylie's vision of life as he saw it in these last, almost desperate years.

This extraordinary revival of Wylie's creative powers was a direct result of the circumstances that produced the book. The idea for a spy story set in Hawaii came to him in 1965 or 1966, when he was at Sea Life Park, the extensive marine life exhibit built on Oahu by Karen and her husband, Tap Pryor, and realized that it would be an ideal locale for such a work. He did not get around to writing it until 1968 because he was working on an "important" novel, *The End of the Dream,* and then only because he needed some time off before attempting a second draft of that recalcitrant story.

The spy thriller, in fact, was written entirely for Wylie's own amusement and for the entertainment of his three grandchildren and the adult Pryors. With "a bunch of amusing if patchy notions," no overall plan, and a delight in composition that had been missing for over a dozen years, he often typed all day in his workroom near the Park. He was not worrying about pleasing the editors at Doubleday or anticipating disparaging reviews and another failure; instead, with his "writer's block" gone, he was "having fun." In consequence, all of his creative energies were released in full force, and each episode which he happily composed did not deplete his resources but replenished them.

Wylie in earlier days had written his best when anger aroused his special talents for satire. Unquestionably, much of the vigor of this novel may be attributed to the savage pleasure that he took in ridiculing the Central Intelligence Agency in general and its director, Allen Dulles, in particular. His grudge against Dulles dated from that worthy's attempt, early in the Cold War, to recruit Wylie for spy work. He disapproved of the agency primarily because he felt that in a democracy no governmental organization could be permitted to keep its operations and policy secret from the President, the Congress, and especially the voting public. By showing Central Intelligence agents and their head, "Axe" Eaper, as both comically inept and ignorant, he reasoned, he might inspire the public to be less in awe of them and their claims to special privilege.

A third factor which explains the high level of Wylie's creativity in this novel is that it offered him an opportunity to express his personal vision of life through the actions and philosophy of his protagonist, Ring Grove. Initially, Wylie had planned to use Grove to satirize the James Bond genre by making his own agent middle-aged, unprepossessing in size and appearance, and no great ladies' man. Then, tiring of that idea, he cast him in the same mold as one of his *Saturday Evening Post* heroes, those mild looking fellows who go around humiliating oversized bullies. But, after the first six chapters, it becomes evident that Wylie has begun to identify with Grove. The first clues are certain rather odd similarities: both men have homes in the same areas, both smoke the same brand of cigarettes, and both are skilled sleight-of-hand magicians. Nevertheless, we are not certain that these resemblances are not accidental until, early in the book, Grove is told by "Axe" Eaper that there is no place in modern espionage for an old-timer or his methods. This scene had its real-life antecedent in 1961 in the office of the Holt Rinehart, and Winston editor who "axed" Wylie for the very same reasons and in almost the same language. In other words, Wylie was writing *The Spy Who Spoke Porpoise*, in which Grove devastatingly confounds Eaper, to gain some relief from the galling feeling of humiliation that had not abated in the least over the years.

However, the really important thing about Wylie-Grove is not what he does but what he thinks about life, death, and courage, and these thoughts make up some of the most honest, frightening, and challenging passages in any of Wylie's books. Grove's struggle against his enemies is a parable of the situation of man in all times. The individual is alone; he is aware that his reserves of courage and resourcefulness are finite. But "to bear what he had been obliged to, Grove had finally found the means." It involved, very simply, resistance with moral courage; it is the task of finding over and over again—in spite of the accumulated fatigue of a lifetime—sufficient guile, fury, ingenuity, and coolness under pressure to circumvent

the foe—even if for only one more time—and to win another victory for human dignity. In a far less dramatic sense, Wylie in his last
years was fighting the same kind of battle—against the knowledge
of repeated failures, against illness, against the knowledge of his
own fast-approaching death. *The Spy Who Spoke Porpoise* is, in
every way, one of his victories.

III Sons and Daughters of Mom

The so-called youth revolution burst upon the United States in
April, 1968, when student demonstrations and riots took place at
Columbia University and spread to a succession of campuses. The
American public reacted with amazement and confusion. The
young people in revolt should have been the least likely to behave
as they were doing. Weren't they the brightest, best educated, and
most affluent generation in history? How could they possibly
engage in such lawlessness? Why were they intent on destroying the
"Establishment" which had given them their unprecedented
material advantages?

Philip Wylie became involved in the search for the answers
almost from the beginning. Initially, he had felt open hostility to
the student rebels, but his immediate family finally persuaded him
that he should listen to what the young people had to say, especially
since he had himself been a rebel all of his life. He soon had an opportunity, when he was asked in May, 1968, to address a meeting at
the University of Hawaii of students who were trying to secure the
reinstatement of two popular professors denied tenure because they
lacked doctorates. He emerged more sympathetic to youth's
legitimate grievances, spent many hours in private dialogues with
other college-age people, and read widely on the subject. Still, he
found much that he disliked about the more radical elements, a
feeling that seems to have hardened during an evening spent in the
apartment of one of the Chicago Seven (possibly Jerry Rubin, who
went to Hawaii in 1970 to help in another student uprising).

Wylie felt that the revolution was important enough to require a
book from him giving his conclusions about its causes. He therefore
once more put aside *The End of the Dream* in order to write *Sons
and Daughters of Mom* to the rebels and to Americans of all ages.
The editor at Doubleday who approved of the basic idea of the book
perhaps hoped that the combination of Wylie's name and a topic of
fervent national interest would help them recoup their losses on

previous works. However, a year later Wylie was still struggling with the manuscript, rewriting whole chapters, revising endlessly, sending it to New York for editing, and then redoing his text with the help of the editor's marginal comments. Never before, not even with *The Innocent Ambassadors*, had he been forced into so much laborious emendation.

The effort exacted a fearful physical and emotional toll, and the more ill and exhausted he became, the harder the writing was. Adding to the pressure were the unmistakable signs of an incipient heart and circulatory breakdown (his legs would suddenly become nearly lifeless, making walking or driving a car impossible), meaning that this effort was his last chance to set forth his ideas in the best possible form.[1] A December, 1970, publication date was announced and then retracted. Finally, Wylie, in his own words, "quit." He had strength for no more. *Sons and Daughters* came out early in 1971, too late to be newsworthy anymore.

The central thesis of *Sons and Daughters* is that there is plenty for the young to rebel against, including American involvement in Vietnam (the complacent "silent majority" of "straight kids" is, if possible, even more of a threat than the rioters); however, the rebels have chosen the wrong targets and the worst possible methods—and for the simple reason that they live in complete ignorance of *reality*. Wylie blames two groups of adults for this situation—the Liberal Intellectual Establishment and a generation of permissive parents.

The Establishment, whose members mis-educate the so-called liberal arts students, do so because they live in willful ignorance of the real sciences—chemistry, physics, and biology—and place their trust in the dogmas of sociology, economics, and political "science"; their psychology is some form of Behaviorism, which denies the pre-eminence of instinct over conditioning. Thus, members of the Liberal Intellectual Establishment were Leftists in the 1930s, believing in "economic man," who would find happiness in a Socialist utopia. The clichés of the Old Left are now, word for word, those of the students' New Left; their utopia is one that has failed everywhere, and they have no other aim except to destroy the present system.

Permissive parents, usually in families where the father has no status, have given their offspring an equally unreal value system. Because these children have always been rewarded for "being good" and not punished for other acts, they have no reason for not doing whatever they wish. Never having been frustrated in their desires, they have not learned to cope with life's realities in an adult fashion; instead, they throw tantrums like the children they are. Never having experienced discipline, they have no talent for the self-discipline needed for the hard and unpleasant work necessary for a person to become knowledgeable in the sciences.

Wylie's confrontation with the "now generation" had forced on him the unpleasant fact that very few of them had ever heard of him—and certainly not his ideas. He therefore felt obliged to try to educate them, and he restated literally dozens of his favorite theses, reiterating the major points of books as diverse as *Heavy Laden*, *Vipers*, *An Essay on Morals*, *They Both Were Naked*, and *The Magic Animal*.

Most of Wylie's new points are in the area of scientific hypothesis and theory. For instance, he set forth what he considered his own greatest insight—an explanation of the underlying cause of the decline of every civilization in human history. Each of them, he reasoned, required the technological exploitation of the local environment, which, of course, was always limited in its resources; consequently, the higher the level reached by a given culture, the shorter its time of survival would or will be. He tried to give wider currency to Konrad Lorenz's assertion that animals learn from trial and success (not error) and are able to do so because they are programed to experiment in ways that have a high probability of success.

Speculating on the phenomenon of "imprinting," by which animals at certain periods of their lives are highly susceptible to learning what they need to know at that time, he suggested that such a phenomenon occurs in the human child before age six and during adolescence. This theory may explain why the ideas, behavior patterns, attitudes, and ethical concepts learned in these years are nearly impossible to eradicate or alter by conscious effort in later years. Wylie, therefore, argued that all children should be exposed at those times to one doctrine only: the importance of being always in the pursuit of "the clearest possible image of reality." He also advocated scientific research into the effects of marijuana; the differences, if any, between the races; and the question of sexual ethics and behavior. Most important, he stated repeatedly that all efforts to control pollution were pointless until a coordinated, world wide crash program of research had established exactly what the condition of the ecosphere really was.

Even the readers determined to see what Wylie had to say undoubtedly found the book very difficult. The ideas in it are hard to grasp unless a person has some background in philosophy, and even then he must read slowly and thoughtfully. Wylie's style is a further handicap. As in a number of his recent books, he continued to set down on paper the mannerisms, rhythms, and punctuation of his spoken English, a style which simply does not convey his meaning clearly even to those familiar with his oral delivery. Furthermore, his sentences tend to be too long and involved for easy communication of ideas. Worst of all, despite the heavy editing of his manuscript at the publisher's, dozens of key passages are totally incomprehensible.

IV   Los Angeles: A.D. 2017

In the summer of 1970 Wylie agreed to write a television show about the environmental crisis for a series, *The Name of the Game.* In Wylie's play, Glenn Howard is overcome by carbon monoxide while driving to Los Angeles after a conference on dangers to the environment; he dreams that he has awakened in 2017 in a strange new world where everyone has to live underground in air-tight cities. Despite Wylie's protests, his script was drastically revised, with many of his important ideas excised and some of the scenes cut as too "raw" and shocking for audiences in their living rooms. Wylie was furious: he had hoped to warn millions of viewers of the horrible consequences of pollution of the ecosphere, but the director had produced merely a cheap thriller.

Congratulating himself on his foresight in setting up his contract with the National Broadcasting Company so that he could use the television play as a basis for a paperback novel, Wylie in October turned out a ninety-thousand word novel that, except in the general outline of the plot, bears little resemblance to the televised version. Glenn Howard's ideas and attitudes, speech patterns, previous experiences, and even his car are really Philip Wylie's, thus making the novel at least a cousin to semi-autobiographical novels like *Opus 21* and *The Spy Who Spoke Porpoise.* Added are long discussions and debates in which the author's views are set forth.

The speed of composition, as in earlier years, was a result of Wylie's complete control of his material. Also, just as in the past, his anger, this time over the emasculation of his teleplay, stimulated his creative processes. He was thus enabled to present complex concepts of psychology, biology, and philosophy with a simplicity and clarity that he had never before attained with any consistency. It is regrettable that this book, his most effective delineation of his major ideas, was entrusted to the pages of a poorly promoted paperback instead of a well advertised hard cover edition—especially since the tremendous expenditure of energy in writing it brought on the acute congestive heart failure and, perhaps, coronary infarction which, soon after, terminated his writing career.

Wylie's view of the future of mankind is terrifying—or should be. He predicts accidents that spill radioactive materials into rivers, killing many thousands. He shows the effect of the continued decimation of the land plants and micro-organisms in the sea that produce oxygen: mass suffocation results as the atmosphere becomes unable to sustain life. The dust and moisture endlessly put into the atmosphere by industries and jet planes block out sunlight: three billion people starve to death in the winter that lasts for three years. The half-million kinds of new compounds dumped into the oceans produce new, dangerous life forms until a "brown wind" of poison gas sweeps the earth and kills all those who do not find refuge in the small, sealed subterranean "cities" that had been hurriedly built.

Even worse, in a sense, is the impact on American political institutions. The country is now more aptly renamed United States Incorporated because the only surviving, functioning organizations are those of big business. Individual freedom is gone. The people are brainwashed into compliance by the government-controlled media; dissent is forbidden, uncovered through sophisticated methods of electronic surveillance and torture; and uprisings are wiped out by the police with mob-control weapons invented in the 1970s. In short, *Los Angeles: A.D. 2017* is an updated version of George Orwell's *1984*.

The sexual mores of the future world are, by contrast, like those of Aldous Huxley's *Brave New World*. The revolution against Puritanism is complete; promiscuity and the pursuit of sex for pleasure only are not merely permitted but are actually required by law. Reproduction is completely in the control of the computers that match the individuals who possess the most suitable sets of genes. Gone from the sexual relationship is everything but erotic physical pleasure: absent are tenderness, affection, curiosity about the other person as an individual. This spiritual nihilism sets the tone of the novel, which is predominantly grim.

V   *The Unfinished*

Wylie, as we have noted, had, for years, worked on *The End of the Dream*. Doubleday published this novel in July, 1972, nine months after Wylie had died and left it in a somewhat incomplete state. The idea of writing a story prophesying the end of man's foolish dream of total dominion over nature had come to Wylie much earlier, in 1968, when he began work on it in Hawaii. The task did not go well and dragged on, interrupted by *The Spy Who Spoke Porpoise*, which was fun; *Sons and Daughters of Mom*, which was an ordeal; and the television play and then the novel *Los Angeles: A.D. 2017*, which was some of both.

Wylie's scheme for *The End of the Dream* was to set down a succession of disasters caused by man's destruction of the whole environment by the vast technology he had created as a part of his dream of "controlling" nature. Almost effortlessly Wylie turned out accounts of mutated insects and germs that could not be killed by ordinary methods, of atomic power plants that got out of control, and of the populations of whole cities wiped out by sudden concentrated doses of polluted air. Although a novel must have central characters and a plot, Wylie had only a series of unrelated horror stories, some a few paragraphs long, others extensive and detailed "personal narratives," some in the form of "newspaper accounts" or "transcripts" of interviews with survivors.

In 1970, Wylie partially solved the problem by inventing two characters, Miles Smythe, a champion of human conservancy who had devoted his life and fortune in futile efforts to save mankind, and his friend, Willard Page Gulliver, whose task in the novel is to assemble a coherent account of the events from 1975 to 2023 which left only one percent of the population alive in scattered colonies that are trying to rebuild. Still, the characters never come to life, and there is no unifying plot. It is, therefore, entirely the power of his pictures of cataclysms which makes this the best of all his doomsday novels.

Wylie's main concern is not to show how nature's laws are being broken and how the punishment will follow mercilessly: rather, it is to present the reasons why man has broken those laws. Initially, there was arrogance: man believed that God gave him "dominion" over the earth; later, his technological advances seemed to confirm this belief. Then, too, there was ignorance: only in the past dozen years have the facts begun to emerge, perhaps too late, on the effects of pollution—sound information to prove that cleaning up the environment is not a matter of esthetics but of survival. The people—in their ignorance of the laws of nature, their belief that technology can cure the ills it created, their determination not to give up any of the conveniences and luxuries of modern civilization, their basic greed—are dooming themselves probably and their children certainly.

Despite Wylie's recurring despair over the end of the world and the slow progress of his novel, it does not sound like the dying work of a tired old man. Its craftsmanship is commendable, the style a clear and forceful one, the pace as unhurried yet as irreversible as the march of doom. No hint of the laborious rewriting and revision remains. It is, in this way, a monument to Wylie's powers of endurance and his will to continue.

In the final pages of *The End of the Dream*, the writer's mood darkens. Willard Page Gulliver, requesting advice from Smythe about his book, asks just how many examples of inhumanity, cruelty, and selfishness he should include; he confesses that he is sickened by these things: "There's so little compensatory nobility, so little simple compassion in these events." Gulliver's name is a final reflection of Wylie's longtime Swiftian view of mankind, and it is no coincidence that his initials are the same as the author's.

This book within the novel ends in mid-sentence when Gulliver perishes suddenly in another new ecological disaster without completing the electronic transmission of his report to Smythe. Had Wylie finally wearied of his book and chosen a clever way to end it—or was the death of his surrogate really an astute prediction of his own fate—the last of the innumerable incredibly accurate prophecies of a lifetime? And what of the despair of his friend, Smythe, when he learns that Gulliver is dead and declares that there is now no hope left in him anymore? Was this Wylie's last word and final evaluation, that there is no hope? Perhaps, indeed, as Hawthorne once put it, "his dying hour was gloom." It would be very comforting to believe that it was otherwise.

CHAPTER 10

Conclusion

IN the last years of his life, Philip Wylie refused to accept my view that his most significant contributions were in the field of literature. He steadfastly discounted the importance of such major literary achievements as *Finnley Wren* and *Opus 21*. After *Vipers*, in fact, he had dedicated himself as much as possible to the propagation of ideas and to the presentation of material that he felt was essential to man's salvation. Sometimes he relied on expository prose, as in *An Essay on Morals* or *The Magic Animal* or the countless short pieces which magazine editors liked to print to show their intellectual liberalism. More often, Wylie used fiction to dramatize his theses, as in *Opus 21, The Disappearance, Night Unto Night,* and *Tomorrow!*

In these works—a dozen or more books—he set forth the theories of Jung and Freud; argued against censorship and for the unrestricted circulation of all kinds of information; campaigned for civilian control of atomic energy and for sane attitudes toward civil defense in the nuclear age; and, during the 1960s, worked ceaselessly to awaken the public to the destruction of the environment by modern technology. There can be no doubt that he has had an extraordinary effect on the attitudes of his fellow countrymen. The fact that many thousands of letters—from friends and foes—were written to him over the years is, itself, conclusive testimony to the effect of his works. He, of course, was not the only proponent of change, but his insistent, iconoclastic voice at the very least gave many others the sense that they were not alone in hating the insanity and inanity about them and also gave them the courage to fight for the freedoms which Wylie insisted were their inherent rights.

Much of Wylie's influence can be attributed to the size of his output. He estimated that, during his forty-five years as a professional writer, he had set down about forty-eight million words and had published a third of them—the equivalent of over a hundred average-sized novels. He was certainly correct: his bibliography includes half a hundred serialized novels and nearly that many books (fiction and non-fiction) in hard covers. In addition, there are many hundreds of short stories and articles of all sorts on every conceivable subject, not to mention movie, radio, and television scripts, a quantity of light verse, syndicated newspaper columns (undertaken on three separate occasions), and even ghost written books, stories, and articles. It is difficult to name any other author in American literature who can match that output of published material—or to estimate how many millions of people have read at least something by him; and, since quite a lot of his work was either explicitly or implicitly an effort to persuade and inform, even when entertaining—we can only speculate about how much Wylie has altered and illuminated the thought process of his fellow Americans.

Nevertheless, despite his remarkable career, his many achievements, and especially his three books of great literary merit—*Finnley Wren, Vipers, Opus 21*—Wylie has never been taken seriously by critics, either during the period of his greatest creativity or now. Book reviewers in general failed to recognize the importance of works like *Finnley Wren,* and none of the three major books has elicited monographs of appreciation or analysis from the academic critics.

The causes for this strange neglect can be ascertained rather easily. One is that Wylie did not fit their stereotyped conceptions: he wrote "potboilers" for a living; even worse, he set down his books at an incredible rate—a short story in a morning, a novelette in a long day, a novel in ten—and he made fun of those who claim that writing is a slow and painful search for the perfect word. But the main reason for the hostility of critics, academic and otherwise, is the hatred which books like *Vipers* generated. When we consider the scorn which Wylie expressed for the whole "Liberal Intellectual Establishment," for college professors, and for revealed religion, it is not surprising that most of the reviews of his works are personal vendettas full of character assassination and slander, misrepresentations of the author's views, and other shabby attempts to discredit his opinions. To put the matter simply, Wylie offended those who had the power to destroy his reputation. After a while, they stopped attacking him and did something worse: they paid no attention at all. By the early 1960s, a whole generation of college students had

not heard of Wylie. They had been deprived of the privilege of encountering the man who had done so much to free them from the
tyrants who had once enchained the spirits of their parents and
grandparents.

Nevertheless, Philip Wylie had done his work well. Those
"Moms" and other assorted vipers who rejoiced over his obituary
notice celebrated an event which, in fact, never took place. In their
hopeless ignorance, they did not perceive the awesome truth: Philip
Wylie lives. His work endures: he has broken their hold on the
world, and there's not a damned thing they can do about it.

Notes and References

Chapter One

1. "Max Wylie," *Current Biography* (New York, 1940), pp.888 - 89. The mother's death is described in Max Wylie's *The Gift of Janice* (New York: Doubleday, 1964), p. 7.

2. See "What It's Like to be Psychoanalyzed," *American Weekly* (October 21, 1956), p. 24.

3. For examples of his support of the rights of women, see "What Women Did for Me," *Woman's Home Companion*, LXXXIII (October, 1956), 9 - 10, and "Why Women Go for Heels," *American Weekly* (August 10, 1958), pp. 4 - 5.

4. See "What It's Like to be Psychoanalyzed," pp. 5, 6, 24, 25.

5. See Max Wylie's *Go Home and Tell Your Mother* (New York: Rinehart, 1950), a semi-autobiographical novel in which Jared Iverson is based on Philip as a boy. Philip's own account is in "Just Thinking," *Ladies' Home Journal*, LXXX (November, 1963), 48, 50.

6. See the manuscript of *Boy Into Man* and "Safe and Insane," *Atlantic*, CLXXXI (January, 1948), 90 - 93.

7. Max Wylie, *The Gift of Janice*, p. 6.

8. See "Why Colleges Fail Students," *Saturday Evening Post*, CCIII (December 15, 1930), 25, 130, 132, 133, and "The Illiteracy of Educators," *Saturday Review*, XXVII (June 3, 1944), 12 - 13.

Chapter Two

1. See the story, "Never Question Youth," *Redbook*, N.V. (June, 1931), pp. 80 - 83, 116 - 20, "Avant-Garde, Number 9," *New York Times Book Review* (June 16, 1946), pp. 4, 76, and "Run for Your Lives," *Saturday Review*, XXIX (February 16, 1946), 20 - 22.

2. These opinions of Sally are based on the recollections of Philip, of Max Wylie (interview, June 14, 1970), and of Margaret Wylie Sydnor (interview, August 3, 1971). Karen Pryor and Frederica Ballard Wylie find this evaluation of Sally to be unjust and distorted. Though Philip may have been unfair in his opinion, it is that view which is reflected in his fiction.

3. Sam Moskowitz, *Explorers of the Infinite* (New York: World Publishing Company, 1960), p. 278. J. Randolph Cox (letter of January 30, 1970) strongly supports Wylie's claim.

Chapter Three

1. "Knowledge for Man's Sake," *Bulletin of the Atomic Scientists*, IX (November, 1953), 330 - 31.

2. This description of Wylie was printed in *Redbook* in August, 1931, p. 24. See March, 1936, p. 14, for the comparison to Fitzgerald.

3. "Mom" also will be prominent in *Second Honeymoon* (1936), *Too Much of Everything* (1936), *Neither Strong Nor Silent* (1938), *Profile of a Prodigal* (1938), *James McVane, M.D.* (1938), *I Haunt a Castle* (1939), *No Scandal!* (1940), and *A Man Can Stand So Much* (1940).

Chapter Five

1. Item in Box 8, Princeton Collection.

2. The serious problems which threatened their marriage are found in Philip's letter to Max, February 18, 1958, Boston University Collection.

3. Item in Box 8, Princeton Collection.

4. See his sarcastic "The Russians Have Beards," *Saturday Evening Post*, CCIV (December 31, 1931), 21, 72 - 73. A series of *Redbook* stories satirized or attacked the ideas of the New Deal, unionism, and Leftist ideas. See "Mogu Bogo Gets the Brain Trust" (1935), "Experiment in Barter" (1935), and *A Man Can Stand So Much* (1940). *Comrade Casey* appeared in *Cosmopolitan* (1948) with the same views.

5. Anonymous, "Crunch and Des Cruise off the Printed Page," *Saturday Evening Post*, CCXXVIII (March 31, 1956), 134. J. P. Shanley, "Philip Wylie on Television," *New York Times* (September 16, 1956), p. 13.

Chapter Six

1. See "How to Admire Writers," *Atlantic*, CLXXXV (May, 1950), 39 - 43, and "The Rascals Who Impersonate Me," *Saturday Evening Post*, CCXXXI (March 21, 1959), 31, 124 - 26.

2. Taped interview with Keefer, August, 1970.

Chapter Seven

1. See his reply, "Liberty and the Ladies," *American Scholar*, XIX (April, 1950), 171 - 78.

2. "A Better Way to Beat the Bomb," *Atlantic*, CLXXXVII (February, 1951), 38 - 42; "Panic, Psychology, and the Bomb," *Bulletin of Atomic Scientists*, X (February, 1954), 37 - 40, 63.

3. Lewis Nichols, "Talk with Philip Wylie," *New York Times Book Review* (February 21, 1954), p. 12.

4. "Why I Believe There Will Be No All-Out War," *Rotarian*, XCVII (September, 1960), 22 - 25.

Chapter Eight

1. "A Writer's Throes, Woes," *Life*, XLII (May 6, 1957), 149, 150, 152.
2. Interview with Keefer, August, 1966.

Chapter Nine

1. The horrible details of his circulatory breakdown are found in his last letter to Max, May 11, 1971 (Boston University Collection).

Selected Bibliography

PRIMARY SOURCES

1. Unpublished Materials
Some of Wylie's letters, manuscripts, and documents are available unindex-
ed in the Princeton University Library. Letters to Max Wylie are
owned by the Boston University Library. His letters to me and
various tape recordings of interviews in 1966 and 1970 are in my
possession.

2. Books   Non-fiction and Fiction
The Answer. New York: Rinehart and Company, 1956.
The Disappearance. New York: Rinehart and Company, 1951.
The End of the Dream. New York: Doubleday, 1972.
An Essay on Morals. New York: Rinehart and Company, 1947.
Finnley Wren. New York: Farrar and Rinehart, 1934.
Generation of Vipers. New York: Farrar and Rinehart, 1934.
Gladiator. New York: Knopf, 1930.
Los Angeles: A.D. 2017. New York: Popular Library, 1971.
The Magic Animal. New York: Doubleday, 1968.
The Murderer Invisible. New York: Farrar and Rinehart, 1931.
Night Unto Night. New York: Farrar and Rinehart, 1944.
No Scandal. Redbook, June, 1940. This novel was published in its entirety,
and only, in this edition of *Redbook.*
Opus 21. New York: Rinehart and Company, 1949.
Second Honeymoon. Redbook, December, 1936. This novel was published
in its entirety, and only, in this edition of *Redbook.*
The Spy Who Spoke Porpoise. New York: Doubleday, 1969.
Tomorrow. New York: Rinehart and Company, 1954.
When Worlds Collide. (with Edwin Balmer). New York: Stokes, 1933.

3. Selected Short Stories (Listed by first appearance; many are reprinted.)
"Agatha's Affair," *Redbook,* N.V. (July, 1931), pp. 60 - 61, 120 - 22.
"*Bimini Haul,*" *Saturday Evening Post,* CCXIV (October 11, 1941), pp.
18 - 19, 116 - 18, 120 - 21.
"A Day Off for Desperate," *Saturday Evening Post,* CCXIV (November 22,
1941), pp. 16 - 17, 64, 66, 68.
"A Good Wife," *Redbook,* N.V. (October, 1932), pp. 70 - 72, 76.
"Never Question Youth," *Redbook,* N.V. (June, 1931), pp. 80 - 83.

"Nothing to Report," *Fish and Tin Fish*. New York: Farrar and Rinehart, 1944, pp. 3 - 19.

"Passengers," *Cosmopolitan*, CXIX (November, 1945), pp. 53, 148 - 52.

"The Reelistic Viewpoint," *The Big Ones Get Away*. New York: Farrar and Rinehart, 1940, pp. 111 - 34.

"Widow Voyage," *Saturday Evening Post*, CCXI (June 10, 1939), pp. 14 - 15, 94, 96, 98, 100 - 101.

4. Selected Essays (Listed by first appearance; many are reprinted.)

"Americans Hate Children," *Cosmopolitan*, CXXIII (October, 1947), pp. 26 - 27, 98 - 100.

"Another Modest Proposal," *Writer*, LXIII (October, 1950), pp. 319 - 22.

"The Doctors' Conspiracy of Silence," *Redbook*, XCVIII (March, 1952), pp. 24 - 25, 90 - 94.

"How to Admire Writers," *Atlantic*, CLXXV (May, 1950), pp. 39 - 43.

"Memorandum on Anti-Semitism," *American Mercury*, LX (January, 1945), pp. 66 - 73.

"Panic, Psychology, and the Bomb," *Bulletin of Atomic Scientists*, X (February, 1954), pp. 37 - 40, 63.

"Pop Is a Moral Slacker," *Look*, XV (July 3, 1951), pp. 54, 56 - 61.

"Safe and Insane," *Atlantic*, CLXXXI (January, 1948), pp. 90 - 93.

"Science Has Spoiled My Supper," *Atlantic*, XCIII (April, 1954), pp. 45 - 49.

"What Freedom of What Press?" *Quill*, XIX (February, 1951), pp. 10 - 13.

"What Frightens You?" *Redbook*, XCIX (May, 1952), pp. 44 - 45, 94 - 96.

"What's Wrong with American Marriages?" *Cosmopolitan*, CXX (June, 1946), pp. 26, 154 - 56.

"Why I Believe There Will Be No All-Out War," *Rotarian*, XCVII (September, 1960), pp. 22 - 25.

"Witchcraft *Is* Hurting You," *Redbook*, CIII (August, 1954), pp. 32 - 33, 84 - 87.

5. Published Interviews

BREIT, HARVEY. "Talk with Philip Wylie," *New York Times Book Review* (July 3, 1959), p.9. Extensive quotations.

"McCall's Visits," *McCall's*, LXXXV (October, 1957), p. 30. Useful comments.

NICHOLS, LEWIS. "Talk with Philip Wylie," *New York Times Book Review* (February 21, 1954), p. 12. Best interview.

"A Writer's Throes, Woes," *Life*, XLII (May 6, 1957), pp. 149 - 50, 152. Brief. Interesting photos.

6. Autobiographical Essays

"Rascals Who Impersonate Me," *Saturday Evening Post*, CCXXXI (March 21, 1959), pp. 31, 124 - 26. Humorous anecdotes.

"Some of the Authors of 1951, Speaking for Themselves," *New York Herald Tribune Book Review* (October 7, 1951), p. 16. Valuable assertions of Wylie's literary values.

"Take a Bow," *Publisher's Weekly* (August 12, 1944), pp. 506 - 07. Details available nowhere else.

"What It's Like to be Psychoanalyzed," *American Weekly* (October, 1956), pp. 4 - 6, 24 - 26. Vital confessionals.

"What Women Did For Me," *Woman's Home Companion, LXXXIII* (October, 1956), pp. 9 - 10. A valuable corrective.

SECONDARY SOURCES

Critical Works

MOSKOWITZ, SAM. *Explorers of the Infinite*. New York: World Publishing Company, 1960. Chapter-length survey of all of Wylie's science fiction.

WARFEL, HARRY. *American Novelists of Today*. New York: American Book Company, 1951. Errors in plot summaries but is a useful survey.

Other sources of Biographical Information

HARTE, BARBARA, and CAROLYN RILEY, editors. *Contemporary Authors*. Detroit: Gale Research Company, 1969, XXI-XXII, pp. 585 - 86. Up-to-date but careless.

HUTCHENS, JOHN K. "On an Author," *New York Herald Tribune Books*. (January 31, 1954), p. 2. Important quotations.

KUNITZ, S. J. "Philip Wylie," *Twentieth Century Authors, First Supplement*. New York: H. W. Wilson Company, 1955, pp. 1112-13. Undistinguished.

KUNITZ, S. J. and HOWARD HAYCRAFT. "Philip Wylie," *Twentieth Century Authors*. New York: H.W. Wilson Company, 1942, pp. 1558 - 59. Derivative.

MOSKOWITZ, SAM. *Explorers of the Infinite*. New York: World Publishing Company, 1960, pp. 278 - 95. The facts were drawn from an interview of Wylie by telephone.

Anon., "Philip Wylie," *National Cyclopedia of American Biography*. New York: James T. White and Company, I, pp. 364 - 66. Best source of biographical fact.

Anon., "Portrait of an Author," *New York Times Book Review* (August 12, 1945), p. 23. Written by an unidentified acquaintance and advocate.

WYLIE, MAX. *The Gift of Janice*. New York: Doubleday, 1964. An insider's view of the Wylie curse.

Index

anti-Semitism, 99 - 100
Ardrey, Robert, 142, 144
atomic attack, 125, 128
Atomic Energy Commission, 109

Ballard, Ricky, 19 *See also* Wylie, Ricky
Balmer, Edwin, 51 - 52, 57, 58, 83;
  co-author: *After Worlds Collide*, 63;
  Five Fatal Words, 61 - 62; *Golden
  Hoard*, 62; *Shield of Silence*, 62;
  When Worlds Collide, 62 - 63
Bataan Death March, 96
Beecher, Henry Ward, 17
Behaviorism, 29, 30, 149
Bernays and Thorson, 33
birth control, 120
Burr, Aaron, 17
business, ethics of, 24
businessmen, 100, 139

censorship, 113, 155
Central Intelligence Agency, 146-47
Chicago Seven, 148
Christian ideals, 20, 24, 98
Cinderella legend, 98 - 99
civil defense, 125, 126, 155
clergymen, 111 *See also* Wylie, Ed-
  mund Melville
common man, 99 - 100
Congressional Committee on Atomic
  Energy, 31
Cosmopolitan Book Company, 35
Crunch and Des series, 24, 26, 76, 83,
  88 - 91, 104, 131

death, 25, 104, 107, 113, 144 See also
  Night Unto Night, Opus 21 (under
  Wylie, Philip: Works)
Defoe, Daniel, 65
Des and Crunch series *See* Crunch and
  Des series
dogma, 129 - 30
Dreiser, Theodore, 40

Dulles, Allen, 146 - 47
Dunne, Finley Peter, 67

ecosphere, 150 - 51
Edwards, Edna (mother), 18, 19
Edwards, Grandmother, 18
Edwards, Ira C. (grandfather), 18
Edwards, Jonathan, 17
Edwards family, 17
environment, 24

Farrar, John, 51, 53
fatalism, 25 - 26
Federal Bureau of Investigation, 84
Federal Civil Defense Administration,
  109, 124, 125
feminist movement, 72, 121 *See also*
  women: equal rights for Fitzgerald,
  F. Scott, 83
freedom to know, 22
Freud, Sigmund, 30, 155

Hamilton, John Gordon, 33
Hammond, Henrietta, 33 - 34, 67, 68
Harris, George, 28
Hawthorne, Nathaniel, 55, 154
Hemingway, Ernest, 39
Holly, Flora May, (agent) 35, 51 - 52
Huxley, Aldous, 39, 152
hydrogen bomb, 109, 128, 135 - 36

"idea-books," 74
"imprinting," 150
incest, 139 - 40
instinct, 98, 111 - 12, 142 - 44

Jesus of Nazareth, 101, 130
Jung, Carl, 77, 97, 98, 142
  theories, 96, 110, 112 - 13, 155

Kennedy, President John F., 136
Kinsey report, 120

Kiskaddon, Wilmina (stepmother), 19, 20
Krutch, Joseph Wood, 142

Left-wing literary critics, 78
Lerner biological research laboratory, 109
"Liberal Intellectual Establishment" (LIE), 35, 56, 149, 156
Lorenz, Konrad, 142, 150
Lorimer, George, 52

magazines, decline of, 131
McCarthy, Joe, 113
McMahon, Senator Brien, 109
Malenkov, G., 129
Miami, 83 - 84, 89, 109, 121, 124
Midwestern ideals, 27
"Mom," 19, 24, 59, 84, 87 - 88, 96, 100, 157
Momism, 61, 83, 100, 103

Name of the Game, The (tv show), 151
New Morality, 79 - 82, 92
New Yorker, 33, 34 - 35
New Yorker set, 34 - 35, 72
nuclear test ban, 136

Ober, Harold (agent), 51 - 53, 76, 83, 114
Ondeck, Sally, 36 *See also* Wylie, Sally
Orwell, George, 152

parents' role, 59, 149 - 50
Peale, Norman Vincent, 130
Princeton University, 29 - 32
Pryor, Tap, 146
psychology, 30

Redbook, 52, 57 - 61, 76
relationships between men and women, 40, 43, 46
religion, 20, 72, 134
Rinehart, Stanley, 51, 53
Russia, 55, 84 - 85, 121, 124, 127 - 28, 134

Saturday Evening Post, 52, 53
science fiction, 62 - 63
scientists, 56

Scott, William B., 30
sex education, 112
sexual revolution, 68, 78 - 81, 113
Slater, John, 136 - 37
Smedburg, John, 89
Sterne, Laurence, 31, 46
Stop Hitler movement, 95, 102
student rebels, 148 - 49
super man, 47, 54 See also *Gladiator* (under Wylie, Philip: Works)
Superman comic strip, 48
Swift, Jonathan, 31, 39, 71, 154

United States Information Agency, 73
University of Colorado, 133

Verne, Jules, 23, 65
Vreeland, Frederick K., 28 - 29

Wells, H. G., 23, 54, 56, 57
Winchell, Walter, 102
woman, "modern," 71, 85
women characters, 44, 86 - 88
women: characterization of, 117 - 18, 139;
    colleges for, 85;
    equal rights for, 19
Woolf, Virginia, 94
Wylie, David, 18
Wylie, Edmund Melville (father), 18 - 23, 25, 26, 34, 37, 40, 68, 86, 133
Wylie, Elizabeth (Morrison) (grandmother), 18, 61
Wylie, Karen (daughter), 77, 114, 146
Wylie, Max (brother), 19
Wylie, Philip: adolescence, 27 - 29; adviser to Sen. Brien McMahon, 109; alcoholic, 76, 132; ancestry, 17; animals, discovery about, 28 - 29; athletics, 23 - 24; anti-Communism, 84 - 85; beliefs, 27; burst appendix, 24 - 25; childhood, 23; college days, 29 - 32; consultant to Federal Civil Defense Administration, 109; contributes to *Princetonian*, 31; crucial years, 26; decision to be writer, 27; deep-sea fishing, 83, 89, 91; divorce, 76 - 77; education, 22 - 27; emotional collapse, 127; fighting spirit, 26; financial success, 51;

freighter trip, 29; health breakdown, 149, 152; hostile critics, 156; last crusade, 140; last years, 141 - 54; losses, 132; marital problems, 61, 67; marriage to Sally Ondeck, 36; move to Montclair, N.J., 26; on *New Yorker*, 34 - 35 oral style, 138, 151; output, 155 - 56; paternity suit against, 33 - 34; pot-boilers, 76; preoccupation with science, 30 - 31; reading 23, 31; religion 20 - 21; search for meaning of life, 21, 94, 97, 142; trip around world, 133; trip to Canadian wilderness, 28; trip to Russia, 77, 84 - 85; turns to psychology, 21, 30, 77, 79; two basic themes, 57 - 58; vocabulary, 70; wartime services, 108; work in advertising and public relations, 33 - 35; World War II years, 95 - 108; writing for pulps, 35 - 36; as young writer, 33 - 50

WORKS: FICTION

Answer, The, 128 - 30
April Afternoon, An, 91 - 95
As They Reveled, 33, 78 - 81
Babes and Sucklings, 31, 33, 36, 40 - 46
Big Ones Get Away, 89
Blondy's Boy Friend, 49 -50
Disappearance, The, 121 - 24, 127
End of the Dream, The, 146, 148, 153 - 54
Finnley Wren, 26, 31, 33 - 36, 40, 45, 46, 61, 65 - 75, 78, 79, 155, 156
Fish and Tin Fish, 89
Footprint of Cinderella, The, 57
Gladiator, 24, 46 - 49, 54
Heavy Laden, 25, 31, 36 - 40, 43, 68
Home from the Hills, 86 - 87
Los Angeles A.D. 2017, 151 - 52
Murderer Invisible, The, 54
Night Unto Night, 25, 104 - 08, 117
9 Rittenhouse Square, 57 See also *The Footprint of Cinderella*
No Scandal!, 87 - 88
One Love at a Time, 78 - 79 See also *As They Reveled*
Opus 21, 25, 26, 109, 112, 113 - 21, 136, 155, 156

Other Horseman, The, 95 - 96
Party, The, 45 See also *Babes and Sucklings*
Savage Gentleman, The, 64 - 65
Second Honeymoon, 83 - 84
Selected Stories of Philip Wylie, 89 - 90
Smiling Corpse, The, 35, 77 - 78
Smoke Across The Moon, 84 - 86
Spy Who Spoke Porpoise, The, 26, 145 - 48
They Both Were Naked, 136 - 40
Titan, 36
Tomorrow!, 124 - 28
Too Much of Everything, 81 - 83, 92
Treasure Cruise, 89
Triumph, 132, 134 - 36

NON-FICTION:

Army Way, The, 95
"Deliverance or Doom," 109
Denizens of the Deep, 91
Essay on Morals, An, 21, 104, 110 - 13, 129, 141 - 42
Generation of Vipers, A, 21, 27, 30, 34, 40, 55, 73, 78, 96 - 104, 110, 156
Innocent Ambassadors, The, 132 - 34
Magic Animal, The, 21, 141 - 45
Sons and Daughters of Mom, The, 148 - 51
Survival, 108

VERSE:

Dormitory Ditties, 31
co-authored with Edwin Balmer:
After Worlds Collide, 63
Five Fatal Words, 61 - 62
Golden Hoard, 62
Shield of Silence, 62
When Worlds Collide, 62 - 63
Wylie, Ricky (wife), 96, 114, 132, 133
Wylie, Sally (wife), 42 - 43, 61, 68, 76
Wylie, Ted (half-brother), 77, 84 - 85
Wylie, Verona (sister), 19, 136
Wylie, Wilmina (stepmother), 19, 20
Wylie family, 17
"Wylie girls," 50

young people: moral deterioration, 81 - 82; "now generation," 150; student rebels, 148 - 49